Power Golf

Drive your Business to Success!

Cheryl A. Nicolazzo

This book is dedicated to all the women who are standing on the first tee, trying to keep the butterflies down, as they tee it up for the first time with a colleague or client.

Welcome to the Club!

Table of Contents

Acknowledgments

Golf, I will always believe, offers life-long friendships. There is no better example of this than what my friend, Susan Bond-Philo, PGA has done for me over the years. Not only did she get me started with good mechanics from day one, but she also became a good friend. Susan, you have always been my golf mentor and a woman I admire for your honesty and integrity. Not to mention the fact that you hit the ball a country mile. Thank you for being such a great coach and inspiration for the thousands of women you have helped to begin their golf journey.

I promise you will also make great business contacts on the golf course. One of my best contacts happened in the parking lot at Woodland Golf Club. Dan and Trish Burger, long-time Woodland members, stopped me one day on the way to my car and introduced me to Kathy Hart Wood, LPGA. Kathy works with players all over the country on the mental side of the game. Our conversations on anger management and positive thinking on the course take up a good deal of Chapter 5. I am grateful for her willingness to spend so much time with me on the phone to help me to describe that critical aspect of golf.

I have had the pleasure of working with many outstanding Golf Professionals in my life. A shout out to Ken Tate, PGA and Director of Golf at Fort Lauderdale Country Club in Plantation, FL. I mention in the book that there is nothing better than a playing lesson. Ken spent many hours with my husband, Nick, and me as he helped me get my game back after cervical spine surgery. We did it all over again a few years later after I had rotator cuff surgery. Ken, you are the best guy and your patience and humor helped me to get back to the game I love.

I also met Mark VanDyck, PGA, during his time at Fort Lauderdale Country Club as then-Director of Golf. Mark was so kind to take the time to read this manuscript and give me the benefit of his years of experience.

At Woodland Golf Club in Auburndale, MA, I have had the pleasure of working with Tom Doherty, PGA and Head Golf Professional. You gave an older gal, with some physical limitations, a swing that works and so much encouragement to keep playing. I have watched you grow over your years at Woodland and I can't think of anyone more deserving than you to be our Head Pro.

Ken, Mark and Tom: you are like family to Nick and me. We value your friendship and are so proud of your many accomplishments in the world of golf and in the golf community with unselfish service to grow the game.

A big hug to my golf girlfriends, Lynn Tennant, (Woodland GC and Palmira Golf and Country Club) and Gail Ferreira (Chapel Hill CC) for reading and commenting on the draft, and listening to me moan and groan about this book. Thank you for all your input, encouragement and friendship.

David Garfinkel, CCM, CCE spent many years at Woodland Golf Club as our beloved General Manager. He is a gentleman who always looks like he has just finished the cover shoot for *GQ* magazine. His attention to detail kept our club house in perfect condition and it was always a pleasure to introduce David as our GM. His wit, intelligence, graciousness and years of experience in the private golf club world helped me to navigate a difficult section in the book where I discussed how private clubs are managed. Nick and I are proud to call you our dear friend.

To all the women at Copperleaf Golf Club in Estero, FL, Fort Lauderdale Country Club in Plantation, FL, Woodland Golf Club in Auburndale, MA and Palmira Golf and Country Club in Bonita Springs, FL a heartfelt "thank you" for so many years of friendship and fun. How very blessed we all are to have the opportunity to be a part of these magnificent, verdant pieces of Heaven.

Not to forget, many thanks to the amazing Carol MacGregor Happy Gatherings, Wayland, MA, for taking wonderful photos that I was able to include in the book and the book cover. You had me laughing and relaxing for our session.

While my husband, Nick, should never be at the bottom of any list having to do with my life, I will stick by the old adage that we "save the best for last". So here you are, my love. Without you, my life would be very dull, indeed. There would be no one to suggest I take a break from the computer, there would be no one to cheer me up when there is a blockage and the words aren't flowing, there would be no one to hug me and encourage me as I chipped away at this 800lb elephant. I deeply appreciate everything you do for me. You are more than just my husband, you are my best friend. Ti amo.

3

Foreword

I am honored to be writing this introduction. Over thirty years ago, I met Cheryl Nicolazzo when she started taking golf lessons with me. So many of her wonderful characteristics have remained unchanged. Her energy, her passion for the game of golf, her constant drive to introduce the game of golf to business women, and her efforts to make taking up golf fun and easy, have been her constant. We have shared an amazing friendship. When I reached out to Cheryl, asking for a book that is needed in today's golf marketplace, and how it could be an important part of every professional woman's toolbox, she said, "Let me think about that." Well, that thinking took about as much time as it does to tee up a golf ball.

We both love to inspire and encourage new women golfers, me with tailored instruction on the mechanics and Cheryl with providing some "light reading" to encourage and empower women. We want you to love the game as we do. Our reward is seeing you make good contact with the ball, great contacts on the course and develop the lifelong friendships that inevitably happen as a result of time spent playing this fascinating and frustrating game. We are always excited when you share news of a great round, a lucrative business deal that occurred simply because you added golf to your resume, or where you are going on your next girl's golf trip.

Since Covid, more professional women have taken up the game of golf. They have improved their careers because they learned how to play golf. They entered the last great male bastion and took their rightful place on the first tee with clients and colleagues and came away with new business deals.

Today, more young women have become PGA or LPGA professionals and have made their capabilities known within the golf industry. They are being elected into leadership roles within their associations and they have helped to grow the game of golf for both women and men.

Golf has been in my life since I was a child. The game of golf led me to my career and has brought so many wonderful people into my life. Last but not least, golf has created cherished memories for me and my family. I hope this book serves as your friendly guide to not only learn the game of business golf but to go forward, break that grass ceiling and become million-dollar golfers.

I invite you to follow me on LinkedIn and YouTube.

Susan L. Bond-Philo, PGA
Relationship Manager, PGA Magazine
Head Coach, Women's Golf, Palm Beach State College

PLAYING ACCOMPLISHMENTS

- 2021-22 LPGA Senior Championship Participant
- 2020 Tennessee Women's Senior Open Champion
- 2019 North Florida PGA Section Women's Champion
- 2019 North Florida Section Northern Chapter Senior Champion (First Female to win)
- 2019 USGA Senior Women's Open Participant

- 2018 Florida Women's Senior Open Professional Champion
- Three-time New England Women's Open Champion
- Women's Massachusetts Open Champion
- Two-time Cape Cod Women's Open Champion

PGA PROFESSIONAL AWARDS

- Teacher of the Year, Rhode Island PGA 2007
- Outstanding Service Award, Rhode Island PGA 2009
- Player Development Award (creating events to expand the game of golf), New England PGA 2008
- Horton Smith Award (educating PGA professionals), New England PGA 2010
- Strausbaugh Award (volunteering to club membership and community), New England PGA 2012
- Patriot Award (supporting US veterans through instruction), New England PGA 2014

Welcome To Power Golf

As a result of my discussions with thousands of professional women, and my own experience seeing how men use golf to drive business success, it became clear to me decades ago that private golf clubs are the last great male bastion, the inner sanctum of the elite business world. My goal has always been to urge business women to add golf to their resumes and take their place on the first tee with their own clients to break the "grass ceiling". In 1998, I wrote ***Breaking the Grass Ceiling: A Woman's Guide to Golf for Business,*** which was published by Chicago-based Triumph Books, one of the largest publishers of books about sports in the world.

My friend, Susan Bond-Philo, PGA, was my golf instructor at the time and she graciously helped with photos, advice and boundless enthusiasm. Susan has made a career of helping women attain their golf goals with superb instruction and a teaching style that is tailored to the individual and a lesson that is never without humor. We have always shared an infectious energy about golf. I spent my time working on my game, building a golf association for local businesswomen, and traveling to speak about using golf as a business tool for companies like Ford, Pepsi, GE Aircraft Engines, Putnam Investments and PWC. I was writing articles on women's golf for regional newspapers and magazines. Susan was holding clinics for the members of my association and helping them learn the rules and the etiquette. We were so excited about our efforts to help women and we were certain my book would become a useful tool for professional women.

Anxiously awaiting the arrival of my book from the publisher, imagine my surprise when my complimentary author's copies arrived with a stock photo of a Size 2, 20-something female golfer with a perfect swing finish on the cover of my book. Perfect if you are a College Division One golfer, but not appropriate for my audience of executive women who are beginning to play golf. The irony was not lost on me. Once again. Men. In. Charge.

While I know I am hardly a household name, this time around, I put myself on the cover because it's *my* money and *my* decision. Finally, Woman. In. Charge.

True to golf's assurance of making lifelong friendships and some good business contacts, Susan and I have remained in touch despite job, geographical and marriage changes. During one of our more recent conversations, she urged me to revise and update my book. She said there are so many women taking up golf now and my "little book" would be very valuable for her female executive "students" and would be invaluable to her PGA colleagues around the country in their efforts to help women add golf to their resumes. Her last comment as our phone conversation came to an end was "Don't pink it and don't shrink it." Always with a bit of mischief in her method, she basically told me it was time to offer a no-nonsense assessment of where women and golf stand in the business world and in the world of private golf clubs today. So flowers and butterflies aside, I asked many of my golf girlfriends who are successful executives, and members of private golf clubs, what they thought about me "Taking a Mulligan" on the book and received encouraging feedback.

I decided that **Breaking the Grass Ceiling** needed a new and more compelling title. **Power Golf** was the winner from a long list of possible titles because power is what women are striving to attain. The power to climb the corporate ladder, the economic power that comes with success, the intellectual power that comes from years of experience and the power to steer the direction and future of their careers and businesses.

The great news is there are thousands upon thousands of executive women golfers, and their stories are inspiring. There are some new Rules of Golf to share and the key rules we need to learn are boiled down here into plain English. The new rules have made golf a little more user-friendly. We don't have to be quite so on edge about making a mistake and being penalized with extra strokes added to our scorecard. Don't get me wrong, there are still penalties, but now you will know what they are and how to apply them. Knowledge is empowering, so please take some time and familiarize yourself with just a handful of the rules. The more you play, the easier it is to understand the rules. Your Instructor and new golf friends will be happy to help you as you begin your journey to add golf to your resume.

There are exciting reports on not only the growth of women's golf, but the laudable inroads women have made in both corporate life and in their entrepreneurial undertakings, many of which are as a direct result of golf. Women are taking up golf in record numbers for both business as well as leisure. Golf is indeed helping them to drive their business to success and realize the prestige and perks of being a *power golfer.*

What else has changed and improved? Golf attire, one of my favorite subjects. The clothes today are so much better. Stylish, colorful, feminine and flattering golf clothes are easy to wash and travel effortlessly. Dozens of companies give us countless options to look our best and be comfortable while playing. I have listed many golf attire companies in Chapter 2 and wish you happy shopping.

Golf equipment is better. Club heads have larger sweet spots and flexible graphite shafts that allow for better accuracy and more distance. Grips now come in a variety of sizes and textures. Golf balls are designed with your swing speed in mind. Even the golf carts have improved with many now equipped with GPS systems, which I believe help to speed play. Short of that, there are dozens of hand-held range finders on the market that give us accurate distance readings to the pin from any unobstructed spot on the hole.

It sure beats trying to find yardage markers embedded in the fairways as we did many years ago.

Players who like to walk now have the option of buying battery-powered carts to move their clubs along silently as they stroll down the fairway with a hand-held remote control device. No more pushing or pulling your cart up steep hills. Unless, of course, you want to get that extra workout. Nothing wrong with that, either.

There are more female golf instructors. These dedicated PGA and LPGA professionals skillfully help new golfers by teaching them the mechanics of a good swing, explain the rules and etiquette and introduce their "students" to other professional women who are learning to play. Most likely, those women will become friends and play together for years to come. They might even do some business together. Well, isn't that the goal of using golf as a business tool?

Post-Covid, American workers were coming out of isolation and looking for ways to be outside together, albeit with a bit of distance. The need for fresh air, exercise and some human contact led many people to the game of golf. In 2020, golf experienced its biggest increase since 1997 with an estimated 25 million players hitting the links. You can rest assured there is room for you to join those numbers, meet new friends and make new business connections. You do not have to be a low handicap player, you just have to have a good attitude and be willing to invest some time, effort and money.

Simply stated, I love golf. It has been a huge part of my life for well over 40 years. Golf has given me laughter and overwhelming joy, brought me to tears of frustration, taught me grace and humility in both victory and defeat and showered me with dozens of friends from across Canada and throughout the lower 48. My dearest friendships are almost all entirely as a result of golf.

I am still learning about the game. Golf is a lifelong commitment to learning the nuances, studying the mechanics and absorbing the life lessons the game teaches us. I hope the contents of this book resonate with my readers, especially young professional women. I hope it helps businesswomen find the confidence to add golf to their resumes and become even *more successful and empowered.* I also hope it might help women who are not in the workforce, but need a handy reference as they get started as new golfers, no matter their age. There is plenty of practical advice and helpful suggestions here to assist you on your journey.

The golf industry today welcomes women and understands their needs and goals. They are committed to delivering the services and assistance you need to make golf your game for a lifetime.

And lastly, I hope the information, advice, anecdotes and suggestions presented here will make golf "the game changer" for your career and will help you ***drive your business to success.***

My most recent book, ***Bread & Putter: Golf, Guests and Great Food*** has been a tremendous success with several printings. It gave me an opportunity to have some fun with my other lifelong passions – cooking and entertaining. Many private golf clubs have used it as favors for Guest Days from Ocean Reef in Key Largo, FL to The Kittansett Club, which is nestled in Buzzards Bay in Massachusetts. Happily, I was invited to play and say a few words after lunch at many of the Clubs who gave the book as guest favors. Often, women who were in attendance would contact me a few days later and ask to buy more copies to give as gifts. Now, you can find ***Bread & Putter*** on Amazon.com. The book also includes two bonus sections: 101 Ways to Improve Your Golf Game and 101 Guest Day Ideas. (At last, Amazon handles fulfillment. Ding Dong. Your books are here.)

Please let me hear from you about how ***Power Golf*** has helped you and share your business golf success stories. Who knows, there may be a future book with all your stories once you enter the world of business golf. If I have missed something or made an error, or if you would like to share your golf story, you can find me on LinkedIn or write to me at canicolazzo@aol.com.

With all good wishes,

Cheryl Nicolazzo

"Make sure that the career you choose is one you enjoy. If you don't enjoy what you're doing, it will be difficult to give the extra time, effort, and devotion it takes to be a success. If it is a career that you find fun and enjoyable, then you will do whatever it takes. You will give freely of your time and effort and you will not feel that you are making a sacrifice in order to be a success."

Unknown

Chapter 1

A Deep Dive Into Women and Golf

At Last, The Glass Ceiling Has Some Cracks

"The Glass Ceiling" is a term that came into being in 1978 during a speech given by feminist Marilyn Loden. Almost half a century later, we are still bumping into ceilings and navigating obstacles, beginning with the aptly named "Broken Rung" found immediately at the *first step* up the management ladder. One senior management woman told the McKinsey Report, "I've asked many times what I can do to get promoted and I don't get a good answer. I hit a ceiling that didn't need to be there."

For every 100 people promoted from entry-level to management positions, 87 are women. The challenge begins as they attempt to attain Senior Management and C-Suite positions. At the top of the ladder, there is "The Glass Ceiling". What does this mean to corporate women under age 30 who aspire to be senior leaders? What can they do to distinguish themselves? Might business golf be part of the answer?

There are some 74 million women in the American workforce today. On the corporate side, the McKinsey Report of **Women in the Workplace** has been done annually since 2015. Conducted in partnership with LeanIn.Org, the report offers a comprehensive study of women in corporate America. LeanIn.Org was founded by Sheryl Sandberg, author of **Lean In** (2013 Knopf)) and former COO of Facebook. Information was collected from 900 participating organizations employing more than 23 million people and surveyed more than 40,000 female employees of diverse identities. Two themes became apparent. First, women are demanding opportunity for advancement at work and are willing to leave for better positions at the highest rate ever. Post-Covid, executives want more workplace flexibility. It is being referred to as "The Great Break Up" and companies are scrambling to attract and retain talent as a result of this monumental paradigm shift.

On the entrepreneurial side, American Express's *State of Women-Owned Businesses* reports that there are more than 13 million women business owners in America today. They account for $1.8 billion in sales and employ 9 million people. According to the U.S. Small Business Administration, women make up more than 51.1% of the US population, and we have grown to 56.8% of the workforce. We have surpassed men in educational attainment, as we outnumber men at US colleges by 59.5%. Women control $14 trillion in assets or 51% of U.S. personal wealth and are now the primary source of income in over 40% of American households.

The Corporate Golf Culture

Many corporate cultures in America today are golf-oriented. In fact, nearly 90% of all Fortune 500 CEOs play golf. If most of the senior executives from your company play golf with clients and your company sponsors national golf events or supports local charity golf outings, then your road to the C-Suite just might be over the fairway. Sales incentive trips, executive retreats as well as conferences and conventions have taken scores of executives (and their spouses or significant others) to exclusive golf resorts all around the world. Do you want to take a seat on the sightseeing bus or do you want to take your place on the first tee? If you hold aspirations for a successful career, golf will help you whether you own your own business or work in a corporate environment.

Currently, more than 6 million women play golf in the United States, so should you decide to "join the club", you will not be alone.

The Grass Ceiling for Women and Golf

Ages ago, there was a running joke around club house locker rooms that the letters **G O L F** stood for **G**entlemen **O**nly, **L**adies **F**orbidden. Forty years ago, when women like me took up golf, there were times it could be a bit frustrating. In fact, it could be downright infuriating. Truth be told, women golfers were unabashedly discriminated against. Calling public courses to get a morning tee time or an afternoon tee time or really just *any* time, it wasn't unusual to be told there were *no* times - even if I called a week in advance. Message: We don't want women on the golf course. Here are some of the lame excuses: Women are slow players. (Not true.) We can't pee in the bushes if women are around. (Not true. They still do.) We will have to watch our language. (Clearly, they haven't met some of my golf girl friends.)

The places where I found solace were the 9-hole golf courses, many hidden away in rural areas and often family-owned. The fairways lacked fancy irrigation, the greens were a tad slow, and the rough was knee-high, but the owners were there every day to welcome all and did not discriminate. I could smack the ball around for short money and put into practice what I was working on from my lessons. At long last, I got the ball airborne. Mere words cannot adequately describe the feeling of euphoria when you hear that crisp sound from a golf ball well-struck. It is intoxicating. It is addictive. It is, alas, elusive. From that moment on, you will spend your money and your time seeking the perfection that the game of golf never grants. Still, giddy with my newly found abilities and head over heels in love with golf, I wanted to join a private golf club.

Are You Kidding Me?

And so, my then-husband and I joined an Equity private golf club in Massachusetts in 1991. After three years on the Social Awaiting

15

Golf list, my former husband became a Full golf member and I was designated as a Spousal Golf Member. In my membership category, I could not play before 1 pm on Saturday and Sunday and I could not play on weekdays between the hours of 11 am and 2 pm. I could not even go to the practice area during those "Gentlemen Only, Ladies Forbidden" hours. But I did get the opportunity to help with the dues, assessments and the monthly bill. Imagine the struggle to get the first few tee times on Saturday if you were going out to dinner that night. Otherwise, it was nearly impossible to get 18 holes in and expect a social life on the weekend. If that wasn't enough to digest, The Grille Room was off-limits to women. Despite my Ivy League education and C-Suite career success, I had to send a waiter into the Grille Room to get a message to a man. It made me angry. Hair on fire angry.

Only one person in a family could be a Full Member of our equity private golf club. That designation came with the exclusive tee times on Saturday and Sunday mornings. Only Senior members could vote on how the club was run. The right to serve, if invited or elected, on the Board of Directors and to Chair various committees like House, Green, Golf and Entertainment was also off limits to spousal golf members. I could *serve* on a committee and did so with pleasure, but I could not Chair a committee. As "just" a Spousal Golf Member, which has been brought to my attention countless times over the last three decades, I am in a lower membership category. Basically, I am a second class citizen and remain so to this very day. There have been some changes recently but progress is slow to happen, at least at my Massachusetts golf club.

The Shot Heard 'Round the World

Massachusetts is known for firing the "first shot" in 1775 which began the Revolutionary War to gain liberty from England. So it should not surprise you that the defiant spirit and quest for self-determination is still well and very much alive here. It was not easy for professional women who were full members of private golf clubs. Finally, in 1995, some 200 years after the Battles of Lexington and Concord, brave women golfers from Massachusetts took their own revolutionary shot. Demanding equal treatment, they filed a lawsuit against their private equity golf club. The suit made headlines all across the country. The intense media attention resulted in immediate and earnest discussions at private clubs across the country to examine their own policies toward their female members. Not wanting to experience a similar legal battle and the possibility of a heavy fine, board members gathered to see what changes could be made to avoid their own legal debacle. The lawsuit filed by the Haverhill Golf Club women helped to level the playing field by shining a beacon on inequality in the world of private equity golf clubs.

Buckle Up. It's going to be a rough ride.

My use of the word "brave" is intentional. Nine women from Haverhill Golf and Country Club sued, alleging pervasive discrimination against women both on the golf course (those prime Saturday and Sunday morning tee times) and in the club house with the men-only card and grill rooms. One of the women plaintiffs, a single-digit handicapper, had her life threatened and her cat was killed. Feeling impervious, the club fought back resulting in a five-year legal battle. In the end, the club lost, spectacularly I might add, as the judge put the club under supervision and awarded the plaintiffs $1.9 million in damages. While justice was served, friendships were ruined and the women who sued were ostracized. Their husbands' businesses were impacted and their golf and social experience at their club would never be the same. The culture at many private golf clubs is unusually homogeneous. It can be a hard road for the one who challenges the status quo at a private golf club. Metaphorically speaking, "the nail that sticks up gets hammered down" when you go against the grain in country club life. Both men and women will shun the person who rocks the boat.

As I promised Susan Bond-Philo, I did not "shrink or pink" this story.

Making a Case for Change

The Grille Room at my golf club finally went "Co-Ed" back in the late '90s, greatly as a result of the Haverhill case. Believe me, we Spousal Golf Members marched in there like Grant through Richmond and made good use of as many tables as we could. Sheryl Sandberg said "Lean In", well we *moved* in. Our motto was "Never give up an inch of club house real estate." It wasn't equality, but it was a good start.

Fast Forward to 2024

Present day, Spousal Golf Members at my Massachusetts private golf club can now begin tee times at 11 am on Saturday and Sunday, and Tuesday and Wednesday have an open tee sheet all day without restrictions. The old Thursday and Friday Spousal Golf Member restrictions (no tee times available between 11 am and 2 pm) are still in place.

What has happily changed is we now have a number of professional women who have joined as "Full Golf Members" over the years. Once they become senior members (a five-year wait and a spotless record), they have a vote on how the club is operated and to approve any major expenditures.

A few serve on the Board of Directors and Chair various committees. In the early days of the appearance of female Full Golf Members on the course during the aforementioned "men only" tee times, a few of the older fellows thought there was some mistake. Perhaps an error, (Harumph) no doubt, on the part of the Pro Shop. They tried to kick them off the course. Imagine their chagrin when they later learned those women were their membership category equals and were told they had to apologize.

Could it be that **G O L F** in this context means **G**ood **O**pportunity to **L**ook **F**oolish? In fairness to those gentlemen, change can be difficult for those who have "done it that way" for decades.

Things like that don't happen anymore at my Massachusetts golf club and there seems to be peace in the kingdom.

In stark contrast to my New England private equity golf club membership experience are the three Florida private golf clubs I have enjoyed membership in over the years. Upon joining, you and your spouse/significant other are Members. Period. No superfluous membership categories, club house room restrictions, or limited access to tee times. It is open, uncomplicated, nonthreatening and very, very welcoming. You can book a tee time, any day, any time. Obviously, there are times not available when there are tournaments, Guest Days and outside events. Otherwise, the only barriers are the walls dividing the Men's and Women's locker rooms.

Golf's Message to Women Today: Come on In!

Today, public golf courses and private golf clubs around the country are very happy to see women coming. They realize that we have considerable economic power and make the decisions on the majority of all household purchases. We take our clients and family to play golf and dine. We buy golf clothes, equipment and take lessons from the Golf Professionals there as well as support the club's social events. We make friends, support each other during times of sadness and celebrate all the good things that life brings like promotions, marriages and new babies. That being said, let me offer one more thought on **G O L F** and suggest that **G**olf **O**ffers **L**ifelong **F**riendships. I believe this reflects what golf means to me and my family. I feel confident you will have the same experience. Don't be bothered with "the old days". The battle has been fought and the doors are wide open for you. Come in, take your seat at the table and your position on the first tee. As Ms. Sandberg encouraged us, lean in.

Golf Builds Bridges

Have you ever noticed how much easier a first meeting is when you have something in common? Having a mutual interest deflects the immediate need to talk about ourselves in terms of our company, products or services. Asking someone what he or she does with leisure time casts everything in the warm light of chatting about things that we enjoy doing for relaxation.

Whenever I would go to a business meeting, a networking event, or even to dinner with new people, I almost always steered the conversation toward golf at an appropriate time. Once people start talking about golf, they are immediately transported to a relaxing place. We can discuss golf trips, courses we've played, professional golf tournaments we've been to, equipment preferences, people we've played with and a few funny golf stories. That golf connection will most likely lead to the opportunity to set a date to play together. By having that conversation, you have started to build a bridge toward a better relationship and perhaps more business. Suddenly, a stranger is no longer a stranger, but a fellow golfer. As a seasoned executive, you know that making deals is a process, sometimes a long one. A friendly round of golf gives your potential clients a unique opportunity to get to *know* you and then they can decide if they *like* you. Then the real challenge is if they feel they can *trust* you. That is how you earn their business. Being an active listener, uncovering what their business issue is, and finding a solution to their problem will make you indispensable and a valued business associate.

Golf Opens Doors

Golf opens doors in the business world that you might not otherwise get through. Isn't that the point of **breaking the grass ceiling**? The networks and opportunities that business golf offers are virtually limitless.

The Hyatt Hotels conducted a survey among Senior Executives around the country, and it was reported that executive women with a 10 handicap or lower (average score 82) earned 30% more than their male colleagues who held similar positions. That is a very low handicap for any golfer, never mind the average female player. However, it is not an unusual handicap for a woman who started playing golf as a child or teenager, played or competed in college and continued playing as she entered the workforce. I know those kinds of women golfers and they are phenomenal players. There is a quiet confidence about them and they are, almost to the person, modest about their playing ability and a delight to watch as they make their way around the course.

Barbara Anderson was a gifted golfer, having started as a kid. She won many high school and college tournaments. In fact, there wasn't a Girl's Golf Team in high school so she played on the Boy's Team.

After college, she went into business and this is what she had to say about women who can play golf, "If a woman can play golf as well as a man, men conclude she *is* as good as a man. They also conclude they are good at their business. I won more contracts just because I could play."

In case you were wondering, the average handicap for women golfers is 27.7, while the average male golfer has a handicap of 14.1. Both numbers are down slightly from 20 years ago so clearly, folks have been working on their games.

Realistically, most of us might never be a 10-handicap. For business golf all you really need are four things.

- Learn how to get the ball in the air from the tee to the green. That means you will need to take lessons. Play with your friends and family until you feel ready to host a client.
- Practice, practice, practice.
- Get your business golf wardrobe in order. That includes decent equipment, up-to-date outfits and clean golf shoes. Show up looking like a player. It's an investment that will pay dividends.
- Learn the Etiquette of the game and familiarize yourself with the most important Rules.

An Opportunity Missed

I have a dear friend at Woodland Golf Club who has raised two brilliant daughters, both of whom are now grown, married with children and very successful in their chosen careers. As they were growing up, she always encouraged them to take up golf, but they were busy with other school sports like softball and tennis. They were not interested in learning golf, even though their parents played. My friend never pushed the issue because we all know how that goes with kids and especially teenagers.

When her second daughter graduated from Boston University, she was quickly hired by one of the Big Four accounting firms. They were so impressed with this young woman that they urged her to get an MBA. They would pay for it while she continued working for the firm. She was clearly on the fast track. In the early years of her employment, while in a meeting with a male colleague, one of the Partners came in and explained that he was planning to take three clients out the next day for a round of golf at his private club. It seems there had been a cancellation by one of his guests and would the young man be available to fill in? It was known in the office that the young man played golf in high school and college.

And in that one career-defining moment, the young man who knew how to play golf was going to spend the next afternoon with one of the Partners and two clients. He had walked through the door of the "good old boys club" because golf had opened that door for him. If he hit a few good shots and conducted himself with humor and humility, he would gain a mentor within the firm. He would have an insight as to how the Partner thought and acted under various playing conditions and he would have established a personal relationship with those two clients. He would be included in future golf outings that the firm would host and have the opportunity to take his own clients out for golf thus further cementing his value to the firm as a rainmaker.

What did my friend's daughter have? A job. A very good job, yet she just missed an opportunity to enter the inner sanctum of the business world: the golf course.

Carolyn Vesper had this to say about missed opportunities back when she was Associate Publisher/SVP, Advertising at *USA Today*, "After being excluded from the conclusion of key contract negotiations that took place on the golf course very early in my career, I took up the game of golf. The following 25 years have proven that traditional business skills are essential, but golfing in business is the single most important secret weapon I've found." Carolyn Vesper-Bivens went on to become the first woman Commissioner of the LPGA. Not only did she talk the talk, she walked the walk.

The Importance of Generating Revenue

I met Carol R. Goldberg just as her book *Members of the Club: The Coming of Age of Executive Women* (Free Press) was released. Ms. Goldberg, then-President of Stop and Shop Supermarket Company (2015 revenue $15.2 billion), was a guest speaker at a dinner I hosted for local businesswomen at my golf club. Charismatic and highly articulate, she told my guests that her book research found that one of the reasons senior executive women were being passed up for promotions was because they were not "making rain", meaning they were not generating enough revenue in the bottom-line, ROI-driven corporate culture.

It seems women are more concerned with "putting in face time" at work to show their dedication and hard work. Men, however, are more likely to take a prospective or existing client out for a round of golf on a Friday afternoon. When they return with a deal, it gets noticed and they get rewarded.

Which brings me to the next point. If you are not in contact with or spending time with your customers on a regular basis, you may not be able to retain them. Nearly 70% of lost customers desert us not because of cost or quality issues, but because they didn't like the "human side" of doing business with the provider of the product or service. What did a globally known business strategist like Tom Peters have to say about getting face-to-face with your customers? "The key to success is *action* rather than strategy. It's all about the people and the doing, not the talking and the theory."

When we begin our careers, we do everything we can to keep our heads down and work hard thinking that is surely the key to success. We get caught up in the work rather than what brings us the work in the first place. Our customers. The customers you have right now and the people beyond your office who may hold the key for your next opportunity. Don't lose sight of the fact that business is done *between* people and business comes *through* people.

No matter how good our products are, how quickly we deliver those products or services to our customers, or how often we "touch base" by phone, there is nothing that can replace or even come near to giving them your personalized attention.

The golf course is the perfect way to accomplish that goal. If your clients or prospective clients play golf, the best way to cultivate a long-term business relationship begins at the first tee.

When the first edition of this book came out in 1998, **Time Magazine** ran an article about women and golf. In it, the reporter referenced **Breaking the Grass Ceiling** and told the story of two professional women who used golf as a business tool resulting in a huge pay-off.

One woman was a Sales Representative for a financial services company. She increased her annual revenue from $200 million to just over $300 million by taking her clients to play golf. Another story featured a female executive from VISA. She went from driving the beverage cart at Visa corporate golf outings to learning how to play golf. She focused on one tough prospect that many of her colleagues had tried to retain, and was able to secure a deal that was worth over $4 billion dollars to her company as a direct result of playing a friendly round of golf and building a relationship.

In my own backyard, I was playing with a Framingham, Massachusetts commercial real estate broker at her club one day and she told me that playing golf with her clients had tripled her income. In fact, members in my business women's golf association were doing business with each other. My membership association represented a wide variety of professions and soon the CPAs, attorneys, insurance brokers, financial advisors and even interior designers and wardrobe consultants were all using each others services. They were meeting new members every month at the networking dinners I hosted or by participating in one of the four 9-hole leagues I had scheduled each week around Boston.

When you are bringing in business like this, the golf course becomes an extension of your office. You are not only working hard, you are now working smart. Men simply consider golf as part of their work life. We should, too.

Here again, the Hyatt Hotels survey found that 33% of Senior Executives reported making their biggest deals as a direct result of golf. Do your clients play? With a little work on your golf game, you can take your best customers out for a round of golf. It sure beats having your competitors entertain them.

As the late Jack Welch, former CEO of General Electric said, "Never let anyone get between you and your customers." He was a hands-on guy with his customers. *Golf Magazine* had ranked him as the #2 golfing executive in the country, just behind Scott McNeally of Sun Micro Systems who held the #1 spot. Today, the top golfing CEO is Chevron's John Watson, who plays to a 2-handicap. On the other end of the spectrum is Warren Buffet, Berkshire Hathaway, who claims he is lucky to break 100 at age 80. Nevertheless, they are in an elite group of golfing executives who are as comfortable addressing the ball as addressing their Board of Directors.

Why Golf

For decades, our male colleagues have been using **golf as a business tool.** When they are on the course with clients or potential clients, they are not shirking their office responsibilities. They are "in a meeting" actively building or maintaining a relationship. The social interaction between these people during a round prepares the foundation upon which long-term associations, anchored in trust and mutual respect, can be built.

I had a wonderful phone conversation recently with my friend, Maribeth Nash Bearfield. We have been friends for years and most recently, she has become Senior Vice President and Chief Human Resources Officer for ServPro, headquartered in Gallatin, Tennessee. (We used to be able to meet at Woodland Golf Club for dinner, hence the phone call.) I called her to talk about DEI, but we started out talking about her company. She told me that ServPro has been a family-owned, golf-centric company for over 50 years.

The Blackstone Group acquired a majority position in 2019 for over $1billion. With a long history of ServPro supporting the PGA and the LPGA, Maribeth told me that the company leaders know that playing golf with customers has tremendous value. She said, "The trust that is formed as a result of playing golf with customers affords the opportunity to have a conversation that perhaps they cannot have anywhere else, fully knowing it won't go anywhere else." Golf is ingrained in the company so much that the former CEO owns the country club where much ServPro business golf takes place. Take a moment to visit the ServPro website where you will see how this hugely successful company is admired for its brand integrity and what it does nationally for the game of golf. They are a shining example of good corporate citizenship.

For many, the allure of golf is that it gives us back the "in-between time" we used to have before cell phones, Zoom meetings and our high-tech, immediate response culture robbed us of a few quiet moments during a work day. Simply stated, golf makes work fun. Where else can you spend four hours with a good customer and spend a bit of additional time at the 19th hole to kick back, review your day on the course, and talk a little business?

Golf is good for you

Did you know that you can burn 1300 calories for 18 holes despite riding in a motorized golf cart? There is still a whole lot of walking even if you are riding in a golf cart. If you decide to forego the cart and walk, the total calories burned is more like 2000.

I was browsing around LinkedIn today and read a post that doctors in Scotland are prescribing golf for older adults. The fresh air, physical movement, social aspect and mental benefits are helping people live longer and happier lives. Fresh air really does boost your spirit and sharpens your mind, which reduces stress and promotes better sleep. And we all know what a good night's sleep does for us. Let's face it, ladies, men are not peri-menopausal.

They don't have hot flashes or sudden bloating, unexplained weight gain and sleepless, sweaty nights. Getting out for a round of golf, even just 9 holes, gives us a chance to breathe and take in some of nature's beauty. It helps us let off a little steam, gives us a change of scenery and a better perspective on why we work hard to be successful. That glass of wine you have with your new golf friends after your round, even if it is just 5 holes, is better than any therapist's couch. You will open up and share ideas, talk about your families and help each other not just to learn golf, but to walk beside you on your journey through life.

Golf is a game for a lifetime. There is never a retirement date that creeps up on you once you reach your 60s. Many couples have met as a result of golf. Thousands of friendships are the result of a round of golf. If you love to travel, there are countless golf destinations all over the world. My bucket list is full of places I want to visit and play golf. From California Wine Country to anywhere in Italy, I can be ready in just a few minutes!

Golf is the Only Sport that Offers a Level Playing Field

In golf, we are taught to play against Par, to play against the course but never to think in terms of playing against an opponent. The psychology makes sense because it helps us to play and compete within ourselves. It is a game that requires the ability to control our emotions and thoughts while asking our bodies to perform feats of athleticism with a club and a small round ball. Golf is the only sport I can think of where the individual player is responsible for penalizing herself for errors committed during a round. What hockey player has ever said, "Oh dear, I just tripped my opponent. Let me skate off to the Penalty Box for a few minutes."?

Golf, far beyond all its criticism for being an elitist sport, is a game of honor and deeply steeped in tradition. My friend, Susan Bond-

Philo, PGA, believes that if you are honest on the golf course, you are honest in all aspects of your life. If you are calm and patient on the golf course, it is more likely you are calm and level-headed in demanding business situations. If you are encouraging to others in your foursome, you demonstrate leadership ability. No doubt you have seen it during your own time on the course with people. The game reveals many aspects of a person's nature. Golf reveals the authentic self.

As much as I complained earlier about how some private golf club's membership structures are outdated and unfair to women, out on the course, there is *complete equality* between men and women of all ages and ability levels. First, the course architect takes into account the strength differential between a male golfer and a female golfer. Men generally have 45% more muscle mass than women. The tee boxes are then placed accordingly. In other words, if two men and two women are playing a round of golf and the men hit from the back or middle tees and the women hit from the forward or combination tees, all four balls should land around the same area on the fairway.

The greatest equalizer in golf is the World Handicap System. Every player gets strokes when playing to make the game fair. So if you are a 16-handicap playing against an 8-handicap, you will get 8 strokes. More on this and stroking the card further on in Chapter 9. So right from the start, women golfers have an equal opportunity to compete and win at golf. There are no 250lb football players charging at us, no hockey players looking to send us into the boards, no baseball pitchers hurling a baseball at us at 98 mph as we dig in at home plate.

All we need for success in golf is a bit of skill, some grit and a few strokes on the scorecard. Once you win your first bet, even if it's just $2, you will quickly see how much golf's handicap system gives us a fair shake and sometimes even a competitive advantage.

Intimidation: Your First Mental Hurdle

During the years I ran my Boston-area golf association for local businesswomen, I was in a Pro Shop one day and overheard a woman inquiring about lessons. She was dressed in a beautifully tailored outfit and was trying to schedule lessons around her work and travel schedule. When she finished at the desk, I introduced myself and invited her to join my group, explaining she would meet dozens of professional women who play. The woman's mouth dropped, she put her hands up in a "stop right there" gesture and took a huge step backwards. "I'm just a beginner," she said, the tension and discomfort clear in her voice.

"That's OK," I responded with a smile. "We were all beginners once. Besides, we have plenty of beginners in the association. They have joined to meet other women who are learning to play and to do some networking."

Still, the woman politely refused and walked away. She had decided for herself that as a new golfer, she wasn't good enough or ready to even associate with women who play. She gave up a chance to meet potential customers or to make some new friends who, like her, were just beginning to play golf. Interestingly enough, a man in the Pro Shop overheard our discussion as he was checking out a new putter and said he would like my business card for his wife. She later joined and became a good friend.

Ask yourself a question. If you were a new employee at a company and invited to a meeting, would you decline the invitation just because you were new? Of course not. You would go to the meeting, introduce yourself, listen to the discussion and hopefully learn something useful or better yet contribute something useful. As Woody Allen said, "Eighty percent of success is just showing up."

Having spoken with hundreds of professional women about mixing golf with business, the one issue that holds some back is their belief that they are not good enough to play with men. Well, here is a well-kept secret: the average male handicap is 14. The average handicap for women is 28. With strokes on your scorecard, you just might beat these fellows!

If you have ever seen new male golfers out on the course, I hope you noticed that they whiff, they go into the water, find lots of bunkers, hit trees and often end up out-of-bounds. Sound familiar? But there is nothing in the male nature that causes him to feel inferior or inadequate. He has paid his hard-earned money and he is going to whack that ball (most likely many, many balls) around the course until the last hole.

I think part of the difference between male and female golfers, at least in my generation, is a function of how we were raised. Even though, for example, I began skiing and water skiing in elementary school, played teams sports in high school and took up tennis and golf as a young adult, there was always the voice of my mother in the background saying, "Don't get hurt. Be careful. Be nice. Don't get dirty. Don't break any bones or knock your teeth out." Am I alone here? Well, that is how some mothers raised their daughters back in my day. (It doesn't mean I listened.)

Boys, on the other hand, have a different upbringing. "Get in there, son. Fight back. Don't let them get away with that foul. Sack that quarterback. Take that guy into the boards. Fight for the puck. Win at all costs. What were you looking at? Never take your eye off the ball. Take it like a man. It's just a scratch. Stop whining."

Is it any wonder for the longest time I would not take a divot? The very act of damaging the grass seemed violent and disrespectful. The teenager next to me on the practice range was taking divots the size of dollar bills. I watched them fly through the air and land 10 feet away, waiting to dry out and die. The horror this caused me as an avid gardener gave me shivers. Today, I take divots. I am so over that mental hurdle. You'll get there, too.

Isn't life really all about risk-taking and simply a matter of pushing ourselves out of our comfort zone? Take a risk and hit the ball over the water instead of going around it. Take a risk and lob the ball over the sand trap. Take a risk and start your own business. Take a risk and go to that charity golf outing. And then stop for a moment after you have taken the risk and succeeded. Give yourself a pat on the back. You did it. Perhaps it wasn't *that* risky after all. It was just a hurdle in your mind and it prepared you to take the next risk and the risk after that.

Betsyann Duval, Chairman of a Boston area hi-tech advertising firm, shared this observation with me one morning during a round of golf at my club. "Men don't want to play with *other men* who aren't good golfers. So it's not so much that you're a woman on the golf course, it's more a matter of whether you are a woman who can hold her own on the golf course."

She added that beginning golfers should stay away from the really hard courses. "They just put too much pressure on a newer player and will most likely have a negative impact on the enjoyment of the game."

Finding a course that fits your abilities, knowing a few key rules, practicing the etiquette and being mindful of the pace of play are all the tools you need to feel in control and confident with any group.

Your one true goal should be to get out and play as much as you can. Have fun. Be yourself. Laugh, and curse under your breath if it helps, but stay with it. Finding people who are fun to play with will make a huge difference on how you feel about golf and seeing yourself as a golfer. Being involved in a struggle together makes being a beginner so much more enjoyable. Cheering each other on, and supporting the small victories like sinking a long putt or getting out of the bunker in one shot are the experiences you will share and will become the glue for your friendships and the foundation for your love of the game.

The Sins of the Father

At a networking event one evening, I was chatting with a group of women business owners about golf and was surprised by one woman's response. "I'll never play," she said through clenched teeth. "My father played when I was a kid and he was gone all day Saturday and Sunday from early morning till late at night. Then he was back to work all week long. I rarely saw him."

I filed that away, thinking it was a single incident. As I spent more time talking to women about golf in these types of business meetings, I heard the same complaint a few more times.

It is possible to play 18 holes in four hours at a private club. In fact, it is expected. Allow a bit more time on a public course. Even budgeting an hour for post-round refreshments and chitchat, if someone really wants to be somewhere after golf, it can easily be done.

It's not that I am unsympathetic to golf widows, widowers and golf orphans, but the reality is golf is not the culprit. With over 30 years in the private golf club world, I can say there are those who tend to spend too much time at the club after golf and those who head home to kids and family.

Make the Time

Another reason many women give for not taking up golf, even though they want to, is not having enough time. They feel they cannot be away from the office that long and their weekends are often filled with domestic issues. As a woman who spent years in corporate life and then as an entrepreneur, I can attest to the value of networking. I did put in long hours, but I spent some of those hours entertaining clients or working with business-related organizations. Being visible at work is important, but being visible in your community is invaluable. No matter the venue, my point is the most successful people in any given industry are the ones who spend time with their customers and get out of the office.

Taking up golf could be viewed just as you would look at starting a fitness program. If your goal is to exercise three times a week, try to make a commitment to your golf game three times a week. For example 1) Take a lesson for an hour on Saturday 2) Practice for an hour on Tuesday 3) Play in a 9-hole after-work league on Thursday.

Here is what one successful personal trainer said to me during a consultation when I asked her about how women can commit to making time for themselves and the activities they want to pursue. She said, "Women's lives have a large 'umbrella of responsibility' in that we run businesses, raise children, care for aging parents, volunteer our time for community service and often look after more of the details of running a home. As a result, we end up feeling as though we have no time left over for ourselves."

She suggested keeping a golf journal. Using a journal allows us to track our time spent learning the game of golf over a long period of time. Noting how many times we practice, play or take a lesson, we begin to see a record of events and patterns that can be measured and evaluated rather quickly and accurately.

Journaling provides a foundation, a documented *proof positive,* that we performed certain activities or tasks to accomplish our golf goals over an extended period of time. Occasionally, we are all going to have a busy week or special events that interfere with the time that would otherwise be dedicated to golf. It's easy for someone to feel that she has performed poorly or even failed at this point. But when she sits down and reviews her journal, examining what she has done over a three-month period, suddenly, a different perspective is gained. Keeping records helps us to build consistency over time and shows us what we have accomplished.

Schedule a Meeting with Yourself

In one of the newsletters I received from *North Shore Women in Business*, there was a compelling quote from Nancy O'Hara's column called *A Quiet Corner.* She wrote, "Schedule a meeting with yourself. Try to fit yourself into your day. Consider this appointment with yourself as your most critical one, and change it only in a dire emergency. Put this appointment on your calendar. Be careful, though, not to choose the most difficult time for yourself. Setting yourself up to miss this most important appointment will only lead to discouragement and delay. Taking time for yourself is life-affirming. It will teach you that anything is possible if you continue the practice."

Make Learning Golf a Company Mission

Take a page from the companies who engaged me to fire up their executive women. PriceWaterhouseCoopers sent 200 of their top female executives to a day of golf. (Does that make it a business meeting?) The group was divided so half had a morning clinic while the other half played 9 holes. The club had two 18-hole courses, so the large group was easily accommodated. I was engaged to be the luncheon keynote speaker. After lunch, the routine was reversed. The women who played 9 holes enjoyed the clinic while the women from the clinic hit the links. As I drove my cart from hole to hole throughout the day, we laughed, they relaxed and they became comfortable with the concept of connecting with clients on the course. One executive kindly wrote, "Cheryl is passionate in her message that golf should be on every business woman's resume." I still have that passion today.

The Honest Truth

Golf is not for women or men who are unwilling or unable to make an investment of both time and money. Equipment, attire, tee times and lessons are expensive. The toughest hurdle, though, is getting over the mental roadblocks we set up for ourselves. Instead, we should be telling ourselves that we *belong* in the club and on the course. If you can master using golf as a business tool, you will succeed. If you want access to the inner vault of American business, golf is your key to open the door. Go ahead, take a swing and drive your career to realize the power, respect and financial rewards you deserve.

Golf: The Game for a Lifetime

I cannot think of another sport where people can start playing as kids and continue to play well into their 80s and even 90s. Even taking up golf as adults, which I did along with many of my friends, we still reap the benefits to our minds and bodies by being outside and socially engaged. There isn't a retirement date for golf. Many couples have met as a result of golf. Thousands of friendships and business deals are a direct result of golf. As older courses are redesigned and new courses are built, more tee boxes are added taking into consideration age and ability. It makes the game more enjoyable, more fair and helps pace of play.

The future of golf for women, I believe, is a bright one. But we must "stay the course" and continue to demand equality in and access to the last great male bastion. By working together and leaning in, we *will* be able to *break the grass ceiling.*

*"It's not how fast you get there,
but how long you stay."*

Patty Berg on being at the top of her game.

(True in business and in golf.)

Chapter 2

Getting Started: Selecting an Instructor, Buying Equipment and Dressing for Success

What Constitutes a Good Instructor?

The very first thing a new golfer wants to do is find a qualified PGA or LPGA instructor. Husbands, significant others and all well-intentioned friends are hereby disqualified. The late Harvey Penick summed it up best in his delightful *Little Red Book* when he commented that husbands have done more harm to women in golf than any other entity. For example, no matter where I play, I inevitably hear a man telling his wife, at various decibel levels, "Keep your head down."

Thank goodness Mr. Penick told the "menfolk" to keep their own counsel. He entertained and enlightened us with his musings about this game we love over the course of his fifty years of incisive observations. He was a champion for women who want to learn how to play golf. He was also very determined to ensure they learned in a positive and supportive manner.

There are many teaching methods but it all comes down to getting the basics of the grip, alignment, posture and a solid swing. How do you find the Golf Professional who is right for you? You might start by asking other women you know who play golf and whose opinions you value. There could be a good Golf Professional near your home or office. Sometimes, the Golf Professionals at private clubs will take you as a student even if you are not a member (yet).

Vet Your Instructor

I would suggest you set up an appointment for 5 or 10 minutes to meet the Instructor before you start lessons. If you are a Type-A personality and the Golf Professional is more laid back, it could be counterproductive or conversely, it might help you to relax. You may want someone who is soft-spoken, who likes to joke around a little, or who will patiently show you a point over and over until you get it down. That is the point of a lesson. Golf is all about the "over and over" of learning, practicing and playing. Good Instructors know we are not all natural athletes. When the grip, stance, alignment, take away, downswing and finish are all swimming around your head, you might just end up feeling like a pretzel. Stay with it because at some point, it will begin to feel natural and comfortable.

Ask if you will receive written material. Will the rules and etiquette be covered? Can you arrange for a playing lesson on the course when appropriate? All of these details will determine the kind of relationship you will have with your Golf Professional.

The one thing you can't buy is trust and respect. If you trust your Instructor, then you will relax and absorb the information better. Together, you can establish realistic goals for your game. Very few people who take up the game as adults get to a 15-handicap in just one or two seasons. Golf lessons are expensive so make sure you like the person you are going to spend an hour with on the range. Explain how long you have played and any physical limitations you might have. I have always thought that golf swings are a little like fingerprints in that each one is unique, so don't feel you need to imitate anyone's swing. It is important to feel comfortable with the partnership you are about to establish, regardless of whether you engage a male or female instructor. It is also important that you are comfortable with the friendliness of the facility. As I used to say to the staff while I served as President of The International

Business Center of New England, "Our members are not an interruption of our day when they call, they are how we eat.".

Who knows, you might become a member there in the not-too-distant future and you will always remember the people who went out of their way to be of assistance.

The KISS Factor

Keep it Simple Silly. Tackle just one or two items during your lesson. It is overwhelming to introduce a dozen thoughts during a lesson. Don't get discouraged if your Instructor has you try something new and almost all of your ensuing shots are horrible. Tweaking your swing, your grip, your stance and your alignment all take time and until you get comfortable with it, just hang in there. You and your Golf Professional will work it out together. And remember to breathe. It's just a game. I laugh at some of my lesson shots all the time. When the kid who drives the range ball picker sees me at the lesson tee, he goes on break. People move their cars in the parking lot to avoid my banana balls and birds find other tree branches on which to perch.

Focus on the basics and feel comfortable with just making contact with the ball. It doesn't matter where it goes, it just needs to go forward in some fashion. Even a "worm burner" is considered contact when you are starting out. A friend who took up golf after her three boys had gone off to college coined the phrase, "It's a rider." It meant she hit the ball far enough on a shot to warrant getting in the golf cart to ride to it!

Have a clear plan of what you need to work on at the end of the lesson, so you can work on that when you practice. Plan for about two lessons a month if you are going to be able to carve out time to work on your game at the range and also have time to play, even just a few holes. Otherwise, maybe once a month will be all you need. Learning golf is a marathon, not a sprint. It happens gradually, over time and is not without emotional peaks and valleys. We learn the game in many ways. We learn through lessons, by practicing, when playing and even by reading golf books or talking about golf with our friends and colleagues.

Once you get started, you will figure out how often a lesson will be required. Don't forget, even the Professional golfers take lessons. The difference between them and us is that they work on their game all day, every day.

Make it a Company Event

Ask your Instructor if you could arrange a morning where 8-10 of your colleagues could come for a clinic. You would be bringing in business for your Instructor and you will end up bringing in business for your company once you get your female leaders using golf as a business tool.

Practice Some Self Love

Be patient and kind to yourself. Try to avoid negative self-talk. It's normal to feel you have a hundred thoughts swirling around in your mind as you attempt to hit the ball. Remember when you started driving a car? It was a little scary at first. When you get in your car today, do you have a list of things to think about? Do you think of unlocking the door, sitting in the seat, fastening the seat belt, placing the foot on the brake, starting the car, shifting into drive, using the turn signal, adjusting the mirrors, looking both ways, stepping on the gas? No, because driving is now a second-nature event. It is easy and you drive from memory and with confidence. That is how you will begin to feel about your golf swing at some point.

Hire someone who will hang in there with you and be your cheerleader. With a good Instructor, there are *no stupid questions.*

Like any other service you purchase, it's your money and precious time, so you have a right to be a satisfied customer. If the relationship isn't working, vote with your feet, as they say, and find someone else.

You Are a Warrior Queen

The hardest part of being a new golfer is feeling like a "Rookie" when you are used to being the "Top Dog". Hold your head high. You are an accomplished woman trying to bring a new activity into your life. An activity that will pay you tremendous dividends in time. The $100 bill in your pocket is just as green and just as valuable as the gentleman taking a lesson after you. Do not be intimidated or feel inferior in any way whatsoever. No one can take your power.

At the Driving Range

Whether you are at the range to take a lesson or there on your own to practice, here are a few tips to help you use your time there to your best advantage.

If you are taking a lesson, arrive at least 20 minutes early. Check-in at the Pro Shop. Head to the lesson tee, stretch your legs, back, and arm muscles as well as hit a few balls to warm up. Lessons usually impart a good deal of information, even if you are only working on one thing, so make sure your body is as ready as your mind to absorb the information. Try to focus just on the lesson and not the traffic jam you got caught in on your way over or what you have to do later that day. I call it "leaving your junk in the trunk".

Start with a few stretches and gentle practice swings with a high-lofted club, like your sand wedge or pitching wedge. Then hit a few mid-irons and finish with a few fairway woods or hybrids and then tee up a few drives. Hitting 20 to 30 balls with various clubs will have you warmed up before your Instructor arrives and your lesson begins.

As you get better at striking the ball, you will notice colored flags out on the range or signs posted around the range that tell you the distance from the range to each flag. Generally, the closest flag will be about 80-100 yards away, the second flag about 130-150 yards away, and the third flag will represent 200+ yards. These are good targets to use while working with the different clubs in your bag and will help you to gauge your distance with each club as well. Even if you don't have the distance yet, you can use those flags as targets as you work on your alignment.

Every golf course has a practice putting green. Your Instructor will help you to develop a good putting stroke. You will learn chipping and pitching skills with your wedges. You will learn how to use an 8- or 7-iron for a "bump and run" shot. These exercises will help you to get a "feel" for these finesse shots. Having a good short game will always be your secret weapon because it will save you strokes.

What is Feel?

I hope I do this question justice. Feel can't be taught, it can only be experienced. It is the sensation that travels up the club into your hands when you strike the ball well. It is the message your mind receives after a well-struck shot. The "feel" is different for every golfer and can include all body parts. A player can use her entire body to get the club into position to strike the ball just by "feeling" what must be done to hit the ball. Feel develops as a result of diligent practice and playing experience that allows a player to make an excellent shot, regardless of the club selected.

"Getting a feel for the greens" is something you will hear golfers say when warming up for a round at a new course. Are the greens fast or slow? Are there subtle undulations on the practice green you will have to consider out on the course? When you make a great shot, you "feel" how nicely the club head struck the ball. If someone has great "feel" around the greens, they get "up and down" to save par or bogie by relying on a better-than-average short game.

Spending time putting from different distances on the practice green is another routine that will help you develop a "feel" for how softly or firmly to stroke the ball. We use our drivers less than eighteen times during a round. Once you consider that an accomplished golfer putts at least thirty-six times during a round (two putts per hole), it's a good idea to work on developing your skills on and around the greens. It can make a huge difference in your ability to score better. Chipping, pitching and putting do not require strength or distance. These "short game" golf shots require confidence and accuracy. When done well and consistently, they will save you strokes. Your confidence will go up and your scores will go down.

Practice Might Not Make Perfect, But It Makes a Difference

If I could insert a subliminal message on every page in this book, it would be to get you to commit to practice regularly. Some people who take up golf drop out because they become frustrated with their lack of progress, saying that "the Golf Professionals don't teach them anything."

But in fact, they are not making the time to practice or play, and therefore are not building the muscle memory so critical to sound mechanics. In addition, getting the on-course experience will build their confidence and result in improvement. The Instructor is there to teach you the mechanics, but only you can absorb the methodology through practice, play and patience.

I'm not saying you have to spend hours at the driving range each day, that would just be unrealistic. If you adopt the routine I suggested earlier, which is to do something for your game three times a week, you will quickly be on your way to becoming a confident golfer. The most important aspect of the game to work on is the short game. The real test of anyone's golfing ability starts at 100 yards from the green, and as I said, you don't need to be strong to be effective. It's where we give up the most strokes and an area of the game most amateurs work on the least. Everybody wants to hit long drives, but it is around the greens where so many strokes, including penalty strokes, can add up. The phrase "Drive for Show, Putt for Dough" should give us a clue as to how a golf match is won or lost.

You can develop a very good putting stroke and get some "feel" by practicing at home on the carpet. Put a quarter down on the rug and try to stop your ball on the quarter from various distances. By the time you get to the course, that 4½-inch diameter hole should look pretty big.

When I go to play golf, I rarely see anyone spending time in the bunker. Don't be afraid of the sand. Let your Instructor help you to build confidence in your bunker abilities. Try this for a good bunker swing thought, "Make a splash, out in a flash".

Here is a good practice routine to try on a day you do not plan to play golf. After your warm-up stretches, work for 15 minutes with your short irons, chipping and pitching to a target. Then spend 15 minutes with your woods and irons. Work on your posture and alignment. Head to the putting green for 15 minutes. Start with short putts so you can hear the ball go into the hole a few times, then increase your distance. Work on both near and far targets so you will develop a feel for how softly or firmly the ball must be stroked to reach your target. Finally, pay a 15-minute visit to the bunker practice area. Once you get more comfortable with sand shots, it won't be quite so harrowing when it happens out on the course. Now give yourself an "atta girl" because you just dedicated one hour to becoming a better golfer.

Practice with a Purpose

Try not to be a robot at the practice range by hitting ball after ball with no particular swing thought or target. Practice your set-up routine. Work on alignment. Learn what distance you get from each club. Drink a little water. For added variety, pretend you are playing an actual hole. Begin with a drive to a specific target, then hit a fairway wood or mid-iron to another target, followed by an approach shot with a short iron. Drink a little more water. The point of practicing is to take your time. Relax. Take a break. Ask your Golf Professional to give you some drills to work on when you practice. Take a few minutes to practice the shots that are the hardest for you when you are on the course. If there is deep rough or an uphill lie at your practice area, give it a try if it is safe to do so. This way, when you have "that" shot out on the course, you may begin to feel a little more comfortable and in control. If you follow this routine, combined with instruction and play, you will see improvement and gain confidence very soon. "Practice with a purpose" should be your new motto. With improvement comes more confidence. With more confidence comes more enjoyment.

For the days you plan to play, a 20-minute warm-up routine, dividing time between the range and green, will loosen you up and have you in top mental shape for a great round. An easy warm-up routine to follow is one that begins with a few wedge shots, followed by a few 7-iron shots, then some shots using a 5- or 7-wood, and finishes up with a few drives. Spend the next few minutes on the practice putting green, sinking some short putts to hear the sound of the ball dropping into the hole. Try a few putts from a distance so you can get a "feel" for how fast the greens might be running out on the course. Finally, hit a few balls out of the bunker and you're ready to head for the first tee. Notice I am saying "hit a few" of this or that shot. This is not a practice session. All you need to do before you head out to play is warm up before you tee off. Or, you can be like a few of my friends who arrive in the parking lot on two wheels and literally run to the first tee. "Conference call ran too long. The traffic was terrible. I had to walk the dog.", they contritely mutter. If you do this with clients, you may as well take up Bocce because it will defeat the purpose of entertaining them with a round of golf. Booking a tee time is like attending a meeting. You must be prepared and you have to be on time. Better yet, plan to be early.

Clinic vs. Private Lesson

I have heard women who signed up for clinics complain that the Golf Professional "didn't spend enough time with them during the hour." That's because there is a big difference between a clinic and a one-on-one private lesson.

The Clinic

Clinics are less expensive than private lessons. Clinics might have four or fourteen students and are ideal for both new as well as intermediate golfers. The new golfers might have a clinic that focuses on grip and alignment. The intermediate players might need a few pointers from the Instructor to put an aspect of the game back on track. Then they have the rest of the time to work on that particular aspect by themselves. It is essentially a structured practice session. The Golf Professional will verbally explain the mechanics of a shot and then will demonstrate the shot to the group. While each student practices the shot, the Instructor will work up and down the line of students, amplifying a point here, making an adjustment there. Each student should expect some one-on-one time with the Golf Professional during the hour, but not for the entire Clinic.

The Private Lesson

A private lesson will be more expensive because the Golf Professional will spend thirty or sixty minutes with you alone. If you are a beginner, consider a thirty-minute lesson to keep your frustration level in check. If taking up golf makes you feel like there is an 800lb elephant on your plate, take small bites. There is nothing wrong with eating your 800 lb elephant over a long period of time. In other words, take your time with golf and enjoy the journey. Work on one aspect at a time, but be persistent. The woman who commits to taking a thirty-minute, one-on-one lesson each week, visits the driving range once or twice that same week to practice what she is trying to learn and plays in a 9-hole evening league, will soon become a proficient golfer. The elephant will get smaller and smaller every week.

"Elephant Stew"

- **1 800 lb Elephant**
- **80,000 quarts of water**
- **2000 onions**
- **2500 carrots**
- **2 rabbits (optional)**

Cut elephant into bite size pieces. Fill a gigantic kettle with water and bring to boil over kerosene fire. Add elephant and cook for one month. Add carrots and onions during last hour of cooking.

Serves 3,800. If more guests are expected, two rabbits may be added. Do this only if absolutely necessary, as most people do not like to find hare in their stew.

(I borrowed this from my book, *Bread and Putter: Golf, Guests and Great Food.* No, it is not one of my recipes. I used it as part of a Guest Day theme. There are 101 Guest Day themes in the book along with 101 Tips to Improve your Game.)

Golf School

Going to a golf school or golf camp can be great fun, especially if you go with a group of friends. Golf schools are particularly good for people who are completely new to the game. For intermediate or advanced players, golf school will help you to sharpen your skills and lower your handicap.

The ratio is usually one Instructor to four or five students, and it's a wonderful way to acquire a large amount of information in a very short period of time. Bring along a small notebook to keep with you during the lessons to jot down tips and ideas. You will be exposed to a good deal of information each day and it is easy to forget it after a week or two. Even though you will receive hand-out materials from your instructor, there may be some piece of advice that needs to be jotted down in your notebook right away. Being able to refer to your notes and lesson materials when you return home will make it easier to recall all the information you received during your lessons.

A day of lessons can be tiring, so allow some time to relax. Do some sightseeing or just take a long walk to clear your mind and reflect on what you are trying to learn. A massage or a soak in a hot tub with Epsom salts to ease those newly-found golf muscles are good ways to dust off the day.

I went to Pine Needles Lodge and Golf Club in Southern Pines, North Carolina, a few years ago with a group of girlfriends. Located near one of the great cathedrals of golf, the Pinehurst Resort, the entire area offers an introduction to the world of golf like no other. Pine Needles was founded by LPGA legend, Peggy Kirk Bell, and the program is called Golfari. Here is an excerpt from their website, "Designed by women for women, every day is filled with instruction both on the lesson tee and on the golf course. Off the course, you will enjoy evening entertainment, cocktail receptions and gourmet dinners. It's the ultimate getaway." My friends and I came to refer to our many golf trips as "The G3"; Girls Golf Getaway. No matter which area of the country you decide to visit, there are outstanding golf schools for women. Spend a little time searching the internet for Women's Golf Schools and you will find the ideal place for your G3 destination.

Don't be surprised if nothing seems to be going quite right in the mechanics department the first time you play after golf school. Your brain is still assimilating all of the good information you were given and hasn't quite delivered the details to your muscles. Be patient. Stay with it and rest assured that it will all click into place for a better, stronger game after some practice and a few rounds. Learning to play golf isn't linear. It is more like a see-saw ride with ups and downs, even for the best players.

When you return from golf school, put into practice what you have learned, but don't give up on your regular lessons with your Golf Professional. Imagine how empowered you will feel when you start to make good contact with the ball and great business contacts on the golf course.

Join a Women's Golf Association

There are many golf associations for executive women here in the US as well as around the globe. Some of them may be local and industry-specific, while others, like The LPGA Amateur Golf Association (formerly Executive Women's Golf Association or EWGA) are national and offer resources for connecting with other women who play. Basically, your local chapter becomes your golf club. Women on Course and Fore the Women are two more groups with national activities and Women of Color Golf (Girls on the Green Tee) along with Latina Golfers Association are growing as well. Across the pond, you will find Women in Golf and Business which offers a robust calendar of events and information.

Once you become involved with a group, your golf experience becomes enriched as you make friends and build your confidence. You are no longer alone in the golf world. You will now have connections and never again have to worry about getting a foursome together for a round of golf.

Build Your Golf Library

Read as much as you can about golf. There are books on the history of the game, the construction of famous courses around the world, biographies of the great players and countless books on how to improve. Subscribe to a golf magazine and keep up with golf news. It will come in handy during a meeting or a round of golf with a client. When you have time for more books, buy a few on the funny side of the game. There is nothing better than a good one-liner when you are waiting to tee off. You can "shank" me later.

Golf Books for Your Library

Play Golf the Wright Way by Mickey Wright

A Woman's Way to Better Golf by Peggy Kirk Bell

Inside Golf for Women by Patty Berg

Golf for Women by Kathy Whitworth

Par Golf for Women by Louise Suggs

A Woman's Guide to Better Golf by Judy Rankin

Little Red Book by Harvey Penick

Five Lessons: The Modern Fundamentals of Golf

by Ben Hogan

Golf is Not a Game of Perfect by Dr. Bob Rotella

The Short Game Bible by Dave Pelz

The Big Miss by Hank Haney

Unconscious Putting by Dave Stockton

Fearless Golf: Conquering the Mental Game

by Dr. Gio Valiante

Every Shot Counts by Mark Broadie

Zen Golf: Mastering the Mental Game by Joseph Parent

The Golf Swing by David Leadbetter

The Greatest Game Ever Played by Mark Frost

Token Chick by Cheryl Ladd

Equipment

If you are going to be a serious golfer, you need to have your own equipment. But before you make a purchase, it might be useful (someday, or maybe never) for you to know some terminology associated with club construction.

When the game was in its infancy, clubs were made of persimmon wood and had odd names like spoon, cleek and mashie. Today, research and technology have given us graphite or steel shafts and titanium club heads.

Golf Club Anatomy 101

In the simplest terms, here is how a club is put together and how it works. A golf club has a long, thin shaft with a leather grip at one end and a club head at the other. The club head has a *heel,* which is the back part of the club where it connects to the shaft via the *hosel.* (The *hosel* is very critical if you plan to hit a solid shank.) The *club face* has a "sweet spot" in the center for striking the ball; the *toe,* which is the front part of the club face; and a *sole,* which is the bottom of the club head.

Each club we carry has a slightly different shaft length and a different club head angle (degree) so each club can do its job properly when you strike the ball. Our "woods" have the longest shafts and larger club head sizes because they are designed to send the ball far and long. Our "irons" get a tiny bit shorter as the number goes up. The club face has more "loft" to lift the ball as the numbers go up. God, this is boring, isn't it? But you never know when this kind of discussion might come up and won't you feel a bit smug to know these terms?

Loft

Take your 4-iron in your right hand and your 9-iron in your left. With the club heads on the ground, look at the difference in the way the club faces are tilted or better said how they are "lofted". The face of the 4-iron is more vertical in design and the shaft is longer, while the 9-iron face is tilted back quite a bit more and the shaft is slightly shorter. It is because of these design differences that your ball will go farther on a lower trajectory and roll out more when struck with a 4-iron, while the 9-iron will lift the ball on a higher trajectory and land with much less roll. I do apologize for this mechanical missive, but you never know when this information might come in handy. Hopefully, you will make good club selections while playing knowing what each club is designed to do.

When you are buying your first set of clubs, you might not need 14 clubs. No need to spend money on something you don't need just yet. Since the goal is to 1) learn to hit the ball, 2) get the ball in the air, and 3) develop a repeatable, consistent swing, maybe all you need are seven or nine clubs until you begin to see some changes in your ability. Once you are able to hit the ball a different distance with each club and are looking for more distance or control, it's time to expand your repertoire.

Good equipment is important to the game, so don't hesitate to make an investment even when you're just beginning. What you want to avoid, however, is buying equipment at the closest discount department store or getting a mish-mash of clubs from your friend's garage.

Let your Golf Professional help you with club fitting and selection. He or she can fit you with clubs that will accommodate both your game and your budget. You might even be able to get a great deal on a set of gently used clubs that are one or two years old. Quite often, a member will trade her clubs for a new set and the Pro Shop will buy the old set and resell them to someone who is getting started.

Today's women's golf clubs are designed with more flexible graphite shafts to increase club head speed. The club heads are bigger, which offers a larger "sweet spot" for better accuracy and forgiveness when the ball is not struck well. Your Golf Professional will let you try clubs from the Pro Shop so you can see how different brands perform on the driving range or on the course. Buy with confidence from the Pro Shop or from a reputable golf retailer who specializes in golf equipment and attire.

Insurance and Travel

If you are planning to invest in an expensive set of clubs, you should talk to your insurance agent to "schedule" them on your homeowner's policy. Your investment will be covered in the event of theft, loss, or fire. Best to check with your agent for the most accurate advice.

If you take your sticks with you when you travel, there is a service called ShipSticks.com which will happily pick up, pack and deliver your clubs *and* your luggage in advance of your arrival anywhere in the world. Imagine eliminating the ugly airport experience of collecting luggage from the carousel and then looking for your clubs in another area of Arrivals. I have spent many harried moments looking for my golf clubs at a "special door" in a busy airport.

If you don't mind traveling with your clubs, a hard cover travel case (available through your Pro Shop or online) will ensure that your equipment will get there in one piece. I've even tucked laundry into them for the return trip home. If you think that is too much information, just wait until you have been away for a week-long golf trip and don't know what to do with those smelly golf socks. Whew.

Love your feet

When buying golf shoes, your first priority is that they are comfortable. Just as with clubs, there are dozens of brands on the market today. Starting out, you will want to invest in two pairs of shoes: a sneaker-style golf shoe which is light, flexible and relatively inexpensive. The second pair should be made of leather and be waterproof. Nothing spoils a round of golf faster than shoes that hurt, or wet feet. If you are a "dew sweeper" meaning you love the first tee time at 7:00 am, opt for the waterproof shoes. The grass is covered with dew or water from the sprinkler system and your fabric sneaker-style shoes will be soaked after the first hole. If you are a 2:00 pm player, the sneaker-style will be perfect.

If you are wearing a new pair of shoes for a round of golf, take your "old" ones with you in case the new ones are not quite ready for prime time. You will be glad you did should you feel a blister starting. That is why we have band-aids in our golf bag, right?

Take care of your shoes, keep them clean and replace your spikes when they become worn down and your shoe laces when they get too soiled. You will be surprised how useful new spikes are as you go down an embankment for one of those tough shots.

I keep a container of foot odor spray in my locker and give the inside of each shoe a little zap after my round to keep them smelling fresh.

To keep your leather shoes in shape, use cedar shoe trees. A regular cleaning and a dab of white sneaker shoe polish will keep your white leather golf shoes looking sharp. When your shoes get wet, don't dry them near a hot radiator or in direct sun as that will damage the leather. Just put them somewhere warm and dry. Check your spikes after every round. Replace them when they get worn down. It's an easy job that takes no more than five minutes. Spikes and spike wrenches are sold inexpensively at all golf shops or online. If you are at a private club, the locker room attendant will handle it for you and your account will be charged for the service. A gratuity for the person who performed the service for you is always appreciated.

Soon enough, you will become a golf shoe collector and have at least a dozen pairs to match your equally expanding golf attire wardrobe. Golf shoes and golf outfits are like potato chips, you can't have just one!

Equipment Maintenance

Once you have decided on clubs, you will want to maintain them properly. It's a good idea to have a golf bag with a built-in club separator. This keeps your clubs from banging into each other during transport in your car or on the golf cart. Also, put head covers on your metal woods to protect them. A putter cover will protect one of the most used clubs in your bag. You always want your putter in top condition so you can sink those long putts.

Be sure to take your clubs out of the trunk of your car and store them in a dry place. The heat fluctuations in the trunk, especially during hot and humid weather, will do more to ruin your grips than any amount of play. In addition, expensive clubs bouncing around in the trunk will not stay in top condition.

After each round, wipe down your grips with a clean, dry towel. Once a month, scrub your grips with a small brush and mild detergent, then rub some fine sandpaper over them. This will help to remove dirt and oil from your hands and keep the grips tacky. Tacky grips feel better in your hands than smooth, worn-down grips.

Buy a club cleaning kit and use a small, firm brush with some mild detergent and water to wash away the mud and grass stains from the club heads. Dry them thoroughly with a soft towel. Finally, have your clubs re-gripped every 6 to 12 months. It's a small investment for added control over each shot. Make sure the grip fits the size of your hands. This is another area where your Golf Professional can be helpful. For example, my hands are arthritic so when I have my grips changed I ask to have them built up. Just a little extra tape under the grip makes them "fatter" in my hands which is a lot easier on my joints.

Golf Balls

As an example of the demand for golf balls in the market, the four golf ball plants under Titleist operate seven days a week to produce roughly 1,000,000 balls a day. If you would like to take a virtual tour visit Titleist.com/BP3-virtual.

Other popular brands are Callaway, Srixon, TaylorMade, Mizuno, Bridgestone, Nike, Pinnacle and Topflite just to name a few. With so many choices available, it's not surprising that many players just grab any sleeve off the shelf, assuming they are all alike. But there are some differences in golf ball feel and performance.

No matter which brand you select, they all have some common characteristics. A golf ball must not weigh more than 1.620 ounces, nor be smaller than 1.680 inches in diameter. Some larger balls, or Magna, are manufactured to make good contact easier for new players. (Just wait for the day you can subtly drop this bit of golf lingo into a meeting.)

The beginning golfer would do well to buy the two-piece "distance balls." Constructed with a hard inner core and a durable outer shell, they will stand up to being topped, landing on cart paths, knocked into trees, and whatever other forms of abuse we can and will impose on them. This type of ball will be a bit more forgiving if you do not always hit it well, and also gives a bit more distance which is something every player desires.

The *balata,* or three-piece ball, is quite a bit more expensive. Its center is liquid under wound thread and the "balata" skin (a kind of rubber) exterior is softer; offering more "feel" for the better players who can place spin on a ball. They also damage more easily.

Don't be discouraged if you can't tell the difference. I have been playing for a long time and still can't easily identify differences among golf balls.

Great care is taken throughout the entire golf ball manufacturing process, which is done in large part through robotics. X-ray technology is employed to ensure that the core of the ball has not been affected by any part of the manufacturing process. Defective balls are recycled in the early stages, but defects found in the later stages of production are destroyed.

Once the balls have come off the production line and are painted and stamped, they are sorted for compression, which determines the degree of hardness. Compression corresponds with the club head speed a player generates at impact. The lower handicap players most likely play with balls stamped with 100, which means that the club head is traveling at about 100 miles per hour when it hits the ball. Most professional golfers play with 100-compression balls, while others prefer 90-compression. Eighty-compression, not available in the balata style, is popular with many novices but may seem sluggish to the more advanced player.

OK. You can file this alongside Golf Club Construction 101. You may need it someday. Maybe just not today. It's like reading the Sports Section in the paper or online. You don't necessarily follow the team, but "How about those Red Sox?", is a decent icebreaker before a meeting.

Dressing for Success

Add this to the verity of death and taxes: every golf club, whether private or public, has a dress code. Be sure you dress like someone getting ready to play golf, and not like someone about to work in the yard. Shirts, whether sleeveless or polo style, must have collars. No denim. Choose a modest length for skirts or shorts (short-shorts are a no-no) and tailored trousers (not leggings) for cooler weather. An appropriate golf outfit is all you need to wear to gain immediate respect and recognition as a golfer. And while tennis skirts are perfect for tennis and pickle ball, they are too short for golf. Let's always keep it classy, sisters. I can think of nothing more embarrassing than showing up at a private club as an invited guest of a colleague and being turned away because of one's failure to meet the dress code. I see many college-age women, and a few who are old enough to be college professors, show up on the Driving Range in skirts that are so short, that I have to look away when they tee up the ball. I feel badly for them because I know they are losing some personal currency. (More on personal currency in just a moment.) The other ladies at the Range roll their eyes and the men snicker. Let the young *professional* golfers in the LPGA wear their abbreviated styles. You are a *professional* woman. Golf is now an extension of your office and part of your image as a business person. May I also offer a word of advice for the gentleman golfer. Do not wear cargo pants. Tuck your golf shirt in and remove your cap, hat or visor once inside the club house. One last observation is the golf course is not your ash tray or urinal. Don't just toss your cigar or cigarette butt on the course to disintegrate. Dispose of them properly in the waste can. Finally, we know what you are doing when you pop into the woods to relieve yourself. Every golf course has rest rooms at more than one location. Be a gentleman and raise your personal currency.

Personal Currency

Currency in life has many definitions. You can gain academic currency by doing well in school, especially with an advanced degree. You can enjoy hard currency from what you earn at work. It's how you got that jazzy new car You can attain relationship currency by having happy and emotionally healthy personal relationships. But there is another currency we might not always manage well and that is personal currency. How do you manage your brand? Not the company brand, but you, the individual. How do *you* manage *yourself*?

Personal currency, to me, is all about earning respect. Respect is the result of how we interact with others and how we conduct ourselves both at work and at play. When you are respected, many doors can open that lead you to success. What are the habits to adopt to garner the respect you seek?

We all know "please" and "thank you" which were drilled into us by our parents when we were toddlers. But what do we need beyond the basics to earn respect?

Here are some points from healthwealthempower.com. It is a summation of *Behaviors and Habits That Make People Respect You More.*

1. **Be An Active Listener**. Don't just hear the words, understand the message. This habit will make you a better communicator. Establish eye contact, ask thoughtful questions and avoid interrupting while someone is speaking to you.

2. **Punctuality**. This habit goes beyond arriving at the scheduled time. Being punctual demonstrates that you respect other's time and it shows you are dependable. It fosters trust and shows you are reliable.

3. **Gratitude**. This is a mindset that can enrich your life and sprinkles something extra into your day. Gratitude fosters positivity.

4. **Accountability.** Take responsibility for your choices, actions and their consequences. Admit your mistakes and follow through on your commitments. You are a person with integrity.

5. **Empathy.** Being empathetic isn't just walking in someone's shoes, it's understanding their steps. Showing empathy for those in a struggle goes beyond being sympathetic and can help you to find common ground to resolve conflicts.

6. **Adaptability.** Don't just survive changes that are thrown at you, decide to thrive in the chaos. It helps you to embrace

challenges and turn them into opportunities for growth and learning.

7. **Integrity.** "Real integrity is doing the right thing, knowing that nobody's going to know whether you did it or not." Oprah Winfrey

Integrity is the moral compass that keeps your life on the right course, always aligning your actions with your values and principles.

8. **Self-Discipline.** This is the habit that helps you make choices that serve your long-term aspirations, even when faced with tempting shortcuts.

9. **Empowerment.** Peter Drucker said, "The best way to predict the future is to create it." When you feel empowered, you will take charge of your own destiny.

We dress to look professional at work, even if our office is a casual work environment. We put our best self forward every day. Things like being polite, punctual for work and meetings, having our hair and nails neat and keeping our office tidy and orderly are all the little things that build our personal currency. When you take the time and make the daily effort to build and maintain these habits, the end result will be seeing your name on the short list for promotions and more success in your business. Always be mindful of protecting and increasing your personal currency. If you take a moment to consider this personal currency list, you will find that golfers live by these qualities.

Fragrance and Fairways

Don't wear fragrance when you play golf. While there is an old saying that a woman isn't completely dressed without fragrance, on the golf course it can be very unpleasant for your cart partner or even those around you. (Especially if they don't like the scent!) There is another old saying that your fragrance should not enter the room before you do, so if you can't leave your home without it, spritz – don't splash.

Wearing perfume to play golf will also invite every bee, bug and flying insect to follow you around the course. If you have a bright floral outfit on, it compounds the felony. Bugs just love bright colors and a floral scent to go with it.

A Great Seamstress is Your Best Friend

Don't diminish your personal currency by playing golf in a skirt that is too short or a top that's too tight. Go for a classic, stylish and always elegant appearance. When buying golf outfits, don't just go by size. If you are a generously endowed woman, consider going up a size so your golf shirt is not pulling across your chest. You need some room to swing. A good seamstress can alter your golf outfits to have you looking perfectly tailored for the day. The top can be taken in at the waist and armholes can be tucked for a better look. Golf tops can also be shortened to flatter your form if you are petite and prefer the untucked look. The skirts can be taken in if they flare out too much at the bottom. I once bought a pleated golf skirt thinking it would look so smart. The first time I wore it, the wind came up on the back nine. I spent the next two hours doing a lousy impersonation of Marilyn Monroe holding down her flowing white dress. That cute little skirt went directly to Goodwill the next day. I don't always get it right.

It would also be a good idea to save the racerback tops for the gym and not sport them on the golf course when you are hosting clients. I have known only one or two ladies that can pull that look off. I am not in that category, for sure.

The fabrics used for women's golf attire today are simply fantastic. Pop your outfit in a lingerie bag on a gentle cycle in the washer, hang it up damp and voila, you are, as they say in France, "finis". No ironing is required. I especially love the suede hangers available everywhere for a tiny investment. They keep the shoulder area of your shirts and tops in perfect shape and you will never see a hanger bump in the shoulder area again. I also buy suede hangers with skirt clips so when I have a matching outfit, I can keep it together on one hanger. I find it makes picking your GOOTD (Golf Outfit of the Day) so much easier.

I prefer skirts and pants with an elastic waistband because it makes it easier to bend. For me personally, shorts with zippers in the front visually add 5 lbs to my profile. It's bulk I don't need, so I feel much better in anything that just pulls on and feels snug and smooth. Make sure shorts and trousers have deep front pockets so you can carry balls, tees, a ball mark repair tool and a ball marker. Shorts with shallow pockets will give you some problems when your golf ball falls out as you are riding in the cart. Why do I know this you ask? Because I have chased many golf balls down the cart path because my pockets were too shallow. Live and learn.

Cheryl's Favorite Golf Clothing Manufacturers

Tail, GG Blue, Jamie Sadock, Golftini, Nike,

JoFit, Adidas, Peter Millar, Lady Hagen, IBKUL, SansSoleil,

Lucky in Love, Callaway, EP Pro, Boden, G/4

Skort Obsession, Sofibella, Nivo, Tzu Tzu

Be Prepared

Invest in a good rain suit, especially if you are planning to play in charity or corporate outings since most don't cancel in the event of rain. A waterproof hat is a good idea, too. Keep a baseball or bucket hat and a wind shirt stored in your golf bag, especially if you live in an area of the country where weather is unpredictable and changes are sudden. You'll be glad you have one when the weather turns cool and breezy on what had promised to be a short-sleeve day.

Rain jackets make excellent windbreakers on cool, breezy days, as well. I don't find them to be particularly comfortable, especially on a humid, rainy day. It can begin to feel a bit like a sauna, but it is better than playing in wet clothes. Be sure your rain suit and hat are dry before you stow them away.

On a few occasions, especially after a lackluster round, I have jokingly said I'd like to give up golf. But I can't because I have too many terrific outfits! It seems we golfers have a tendency to collect the whole nine yards of tops, bottoms, shoes, visors, hats and jackets. Don't hesitate to keep a jacket on when you are warming up at the range, particularly if you like to get an early morning start when it might be cool. Aside from looking smart, they keep your muscles warm, which may help to prevent an injury while swinging. A jacket might also come in handy on the 19th Hole if the A/C is on inside the club house.

Golf Accessories

Hats, visors, and sunglasses are a matter of personal preference. Some people can't play with them, others can't play without them. I am of the latter conviction. While visors are stylish and provide shade for your eyes, hats protect your hair, scalp and ears from sun and wind damage in addition to providing a bit more protection for your eyes and face. If you have ever seen the aftermath of Mohs surgery to remove skin cancer, you will quickly be onboard with every measure of sun protection. Tuck up long hair under a hat or use a hair clip to keep it from blowing in your face and distracting you. As a professional woman, you are always looking for ways to stay polished.

Sunglasses protect your eyes from the sun's damaging UV rays and the wind and will prevent dust irritation if you are riding in a golf cart with the windshield down, especially if you are following another cart along a dusty path. Sunglasses will also allow you to privately roll your eyes after you hit a bad shot. Top this all off with a high-level sunscreen on your face, my favorite is LaRoche Posay, some sunscreen lip balm, a mist of sunscreen spray on your arms and legs, a positive outlook and you're ready to hit the links.

It's a good idea to buy a few golf gloves, one for playing and a couple to keep in your bag as a backup. A dry glove for the back nine on a drizzly or blistering hot day will be most appreciated. If you are the fastidious type, use a plastic glove shaper to keep your glove fitting properly. If you are a bit more casual, just drop a ball into your glove to help keep its shape. If you're like me, just drop it into your golf bag pocket. See ya later. I'm heading for the 19th hole.

If you live in the cooler climates where late fall and early spring golf often produce temperatures in the low fifties or forties, a pair of winter golf gloves is a joy. (May I be perfectly frank here? I no longer play in those temperatures or in the rain, but you do you.) Ask your Pro Shop to order a pair for you if they don't have them in stock. Be sure to replace worn or soiled golf gloves. Did you know your golf glove can tell your Instructor quite a bit about your grip? If your glove is wearing out on the pad of your hand, instead of along your "life-line," your grip may be incorrect. Check with your Instructor and get it fixed. My final thought on golf gloves is to consider wearing rain gloves on hot and humid days. I readily admit my hands get sweaty on those days and I find the rain gloves give me better control of the club. To the best of my knowledge, they only come in black. Fashion be damned, try them and see if they help. Those black rain gloves helped me to win my northern club Senior Women's Championship a few years ago. We played in 103-degree heat for three days of medal play. Was it worth it just to hold a big piece of crystal? Absolutely.

"Golf is not one of those occupations in which you soon learn your level. There is no shape nor size of body, no awkwardness nor ungainliness, which puts good golf beyond one's reach. There are good golfers with spectacles, with one eye, with one leg, even with one arm. It is not the youthful alone who have cause to hope.

Beginners in middle age have become great, and more wonderful still after many years of patient duffering, there may be a rift in the clouds. Some pet vice which has been clung to as a virtue may be abandoned, and the fifth-class player bursts upon the world as a medal winner. In golf, whilst there is life, there is hope.

Sir Walter Simpson from *"The Art of Golf"*

What's in Your Golf Bag?

Business cards

Extra Sleeves of Golf Balls   Felt Tip Pen

Golf Towel   Hand Warmers

Feminine Care Products

Winter gloves   Rain gloves   Extra golf gloves

Aspirin Tylenol Aleve

Insect Repellent   Contact Lens Solution

Snacks   Umbrella   Safety Pin

Extra Batteries for Range Finder

Extra Pair of Socks

Tees, Pencils and Plastic Ball Markers

Bee Sting/Bug Bite Salve   Nail File

Water bottle   Sunscreen (30+)   Tissues

Wet Wipes   Hand Sanitizer

Band aids   Neosporin

Rain Hat   Wind Shirt

Several Dollar Bills to pay for Birdies, to tip the

Snack Shack Attendant or the Beverage Cart Driver

The Well-Stocked Locker

Rain Suit

Visors, Baseball and Bucket Hats

Make-up Bag   Hair Brush

Clean, dry golf outfit

Extra shoes and socks   Warm Jacket

Knit Hat Cart Blanket

"Golf is 20 percent mechanics and technique. The other 80 percent is philosophy, humor, tragedy, romance, melodrama, companionship, camaraderie, cussedness and conversation."

Grantland Rice

Chapter 3

The Business Golf Network

Golf is Now a Part of Your Professional Life

Some of the largest corporate mergers in the history of American business have happened on the golf course. Some of the strongest business relationships have been forged on the golf course. The direction of industries, the creation of dynamic foundations and community initiatives that have helped thousands of people have all happened as a result of golf. Without a doubt, golf is a game of connections. Golf will expand your network and put you in front of new potential customers.

Even those of us who are not Captains of Industry (at least not yet) realize that golfers are just ordinary people who show respect for one another, respect for the environment in which they play, and respect for the honorable traditions that are associated with golf. Golf is, at its very core, a game of honor. Therefore, we are responsible for policing our conduct out there on the course. It is, in fact, the only game I can think of where players call penalties on themselves. Golf reveals the authentic person whether you are the host or the guest and whether your handicap is 5 or 25.

When you can offer a prospective customer something he or she loves, like a round of golf, then you are one step closer to building the relationship that will earn their trust and respect. Ultimately, you may earn the right to ask for their business. Imagine a four hour, one-on-one, outdoor meeting without a cell phone, Power Point, white board, video presentation (yawn) or anything else other than two people walking and talking. There is no other activity that pays dividends to a company like golf when the end result is a deal. So let's get your business on course and get you ready to become a *power golfer*.

When going to your initial meeting with a prospective client, you will want to be looking for signs of golf in the office. Is there a picture of a beaming foursome at Pebble Beach, a crystal golf ball paperweight on the desk or a few antique golf clubs standing in a corner? Those are sure signs that you are meeting with a golfer.

We all know from Sales 101 that most people like to talk about themselves. Early in the conversation, you might comment, "Oh, I see you're a golfer. Where do you like to play?".

You will soon find out where your prospective client resides on the golf spectrum: new golfer, intermediate or advanced player. Your potential client might tell you if he or she belongs to a private club. If you also belong to a private club, this is a good time to share that information. The intermediate to avid golfer might be a good prospect for an 18-hole outing invitation. A beginning golfer might be happier with something more in line with her current ability. You could invite her to a 9-hole Executive course or an invitation to a clinic that you are hosting. You need to take the temperature of the situation and determine what will get you onto her radar screen.

The Beginner Golfer

When you are meeting with a beginner golfer, go easy. If your home course is too hard for even just playing 9 holes, go to a Mom and Pop 9-hole course or an Executive 9-hole course and agree you are just there to have fun. A scramble format is a quick way to build a team mentality. It takes the pressure off her to perform well and lets you focus on building your relationship in a relaxed atmosphere. If she isn't ready to play or is just taking lessons and has not been on a golf course yet, suggest a trip to Topgolf. Topgolf is fast spreading across the country and might be the perfect venue for you and a client. (It is also a great venue for team building within your company.) Topgolf has a casual setting with an indoor driving range. The golf balls have chips in them and the targets have sensors. Hit some balls, have a bite to eat and get to know your customer. You can do this after work or on a weekend, making it easier for someone who is hesitant about golf.

Another thought would be to host an hour-long clinic with your Golf Professional and invite the Beginners on your "potential big new client" list. Limit it to 6 guests or less so you can spend time with each of them. Offer a lunch or dinner afterward. You are providing a brief lesson and helping your guests meet other new golfers while expanding your business network. This is a pricey investment, so your guests need to be the decision-makers and people you strongly believe you can secure as clients. If you can help these ladies feel comfortable about golf, they will be your friends forever.

Let me share a bit of additional information about TopGolf. Earlier in the book, I mentioned the concept of good corporate citizenship. TopGolf is another excellent example. They partner with the Make-a-Wish Foundation, The First Tee, which teaches kids the game of golf with a life skills curriculum, and the Special Olympics. They also established Bunkers in Baghdad which translates into over 10 years of service providing 227,000 golf clubs, 98,000 golf balls and 2,800 yards of turf to US troops stationed overseas.

The Intermediate Golfer

I was looking for a fourth person to fill out my foursome to play in a charity outing to benefit a battered women's shelter. I called a new-to-golf friend who was then a Vice President for Small Business Banking at a BankBoston branch in Wellesley, Massachusetts. I invited her to round out the foursome. The branch of the bank was part of the community served by the shelter, and I thought it would give her some good exposure.

At first, she declined, saying she didn't think she was good enough at golf yet to join us. "Nonsense," I told her. "You're playing in a 9-hole league every week, I know you've just finished a few clinics with Susan Bond-Philo, it's a scramble format, and it's for a great cause."

"You're right," she replied. "I really want to do this," and accepted my invitation. Needless to say, we had a great day and my timid friend sank some unbelievably long putts for our team. She also made several promising business contacts at the reception that followed. I might add that her self-confidence as a power golfer went up a few notches, too. She phoned me the next day and was so excited and happy she went. She pushed herself out of her comfort zone and now she was ready to do more with business golf on her own.

The key here is I made sure it was a format where she would be comfortable and have a fun experience while being seen in her community. I was her mentor and it was my job to help her gain more confidence to combine golf and business.

The Seasoned Golfer

Gail Ferreira, Executive Coach/CEO, Lead Succeed, grew up playing golf with her parents in Lexington, Massachusetts and shared this with me, "I found that hosting customers for a round of golf at my club in Chapel Hill, NC, has greatly enhanced my business relationships. The fact I can share, at the appropriate time, that I have had a "hole-in-one" twice somehow elevates my status in their eyes." These seasoned players can be invited to any form of golf; a quiet round at your club, as a guest for your club's guest day, or any corporate or charity event you feel they might enjoy.

The On the Course Job Interview

Some senior executives now take high-level prospective hires out for a round of golf so they can observe how these people conduct themselves during and after the round. Golf reveals quite a bit about people in terms of personality traits. When I play golf with others, I observe their ability to make decisions, their willingness to take risks, whether they are able to laugh at mistakes, how quick they are to anger, and if they are good sports about gentle ribbing.

Susan Bond-Philo, PGA, told me she has had several on-course playing interviews. "I played some of my best golf during these rounds," she said. That is how she recently became Head Coach for Women's Golf, after a national search, at Palm Beach State College in Florida.

You can meet people at conventions, on airplanes, through associations, and dozens of other traditional business situations, and you might forget them in a week or two. But I will always remember someone with whom I have played golf. There is no doubt in my mind that golf helps to create a unique bond between people. The game allows us to connect and see each other as humans and how we represent our personal and corporate brands when we play.

Get Involved in Your Community

Now that you are thinking about golf as a business tool, you may begin to look at your current customers as potential golf guests instead of just customers. There are other ways you can expand your client base through golf, as well. One way to meet more potential clients who play golf is to become involved in a community activity that you enjoy. Museums, opera, symphony, ballet, and other performing arts and cultural events are always looking for smart people to help support their efforts. Tickets to athletic events or attending benefit dinners are all excellent vehicles for making new contacts. Becoming involved in activities beyond the scope of what your company does is an effective way to become known to a larger audience. You will be able to demonstrate your outstanding sales, marketing, planning, or research skills to leaders in other industries, which may have a positive impact on the growth of your business and your future success.

It's not surprising that the group of business people who shape the political, cultural, and economic direction of a community have avid golfers among their ranks. They support many of the institutions and activities listed above while underwriting cultural events and attracting conventions and expositions to their cities. They also invite investors to build and expand the business landscape. These powerful CEOs keep a pulse on events and information far beyond their own companies.

If we conducted a survey of how many members of this elite business group are also members of private golf or country clubs, you would find that the majority of these leaders are tied to golf. When you enter the business arena as a golfer, you are plugging into a very large network. The old adage, "It's not what you know, it's who you know," rings true for the executive who can use golf as a business tool. Inviting someone with whom you have worked on a project for a round of golf could bring you closer to making a deal. Playing golf is one of the fastest ways to broaden your network and gain access to the power base in your industry and your community.

When are You Ready to Invite a Business Associate to Play Golf?

You are ready to host a round of golf once you begin to average around 115 to 125 for 18 holes, can play your round in four hours or less, and have familiarized yourself with the key rules and etiquette of the game. There is an unspoken agreement that a knowledge of the rules and etiquette is the most important thing to have mastered if you want to be taken seriously. Start out easy by inviting just one client to play as your guest at a charity event with a Scramble format. There is no pressure on either of you. Take it easy until you become more comfortable with an 18-hole round that is not a Scramble.

Develop Your Business Golf IQ

Your Business Golf IQ is all about how you manage the golf experience for your client. While you're becoming more proficient at golf and you are playing with confidence and a bit more consistency, you can also work on your Business Golf IQ.

While you may think your course is the best and everyone wants to play it, your first responsibility is to "qualify" your guests to afford *them* the best possible experience. Find out as much as you can about your guest's ability and attitude about golf so you can make the day productive and memorable. Your ability to take your client's "golf temperature" will do much to direct the enjoyment of the day and how your relationship develops. Does your client like to play 9 or 18 holes? Will they play on a very hot day or a very chilly day? Do they like to speed around the course or are they more methodical? Your most important consideration is to make sure you are inviting the decision maker.

Don't invite a rocket scientist to play with a rock star. By that I mean there are some players who are highly analytical and will want to have every iota of data before making a shot during a deeply-focused round. Then there are the "drive for show" folks who want music in the cart, some betting action and a super-fast round. Putting these two in a foursome is like trying to blend oil and water and is a sure recipe for disaster. My point is vetting golf personality types is as important as your playing ability if you are going to successfully host a round of golf. There needs to be some commonality to ensure a great experience. Find out what tees they prefer. You already know the rock star is playing from the tips. Maybe the rocket scientist prefers the middle tees. You want your guest/s to have fun during your four-hour outdoor meeting. If you don't get the personality aspects, as well as the abilities of your guests matched correctly, your time and money will be wasted. Think about Judge Smails (Ted Knight) and Al Czervik (Rodney Dangerfield) in Caddyshack. There is a prime example of oil and water without a doubt.

We can sit in a meeting with these two personalities because the constraints of office decorum will most likely keep them in line. But once some folks get on the golf course, things can be more unpredictable and emotional. You have to have a game plan to make sure your round goes smoothly and it gives you the most bang for your buck. If you spend your time babysitting or refereeing between two ill-matched guests, you have lost at the business golf game. Remember, business golf is not about the lowest score, it is about providing a memorable day, building a relationship based on trust and respect and ultimately closing the deal.

The golfer with a high Business Golf IQ makes the day run smoothly, can play with the most avid golfer and keep up or host a new golfer and make it feel easy. Your Business Golf IQ helps you to anticipate anything that might go wrong and have that all-important backup plan. At the top of your "to-do" list is to determine what you want to accomplish with this round of golf. Is this a "getting to know you" outing, or is this the time to talk some business and close the deal. It doesn't matter who hits the longest drive or sinks the longest putt. What does matter when you play is being an active listener. If you do all the talking, then you won't hear what they need. Ask thoughtful questions. Can you help to solve a problem and take immediate action to deliver what is needed in terms of product or service? Never underestimate the importance of just being yourself. People like to be with nice people, especially during a round of golf. Be empathetic if your guest hits a bad shot. Take your cue from how your guests conduct themselves. Be confident in your game and always show respect for the course. Fill those divots and repair those ball marks. How you conduct yourself on the golf course and around the club house will be noticed and evaluated.

Personal Belongings While Playing

It is very important that you take care of your valuables, particularly your jewelry, when playing golf, especially if you plan to walk. My best advice is don't wear your diamond rings and fine watches and bracelets while playing. In fact, my jeweler strongly urged me never to wear my good jewelry while playing, saying the vibration from the impact of the club hitting the ball could affect the movement of my watch and perhaps even disturb the prongs on my engagement ring. I don't wear jewelry to play golf. I don't want the distraction. But I admit that after a Member-Guest or 9 Hole Scotch, I like to glam up after the round. I have a velvet-lined pouch with a zipper where my finery goes and stays in my handbag until after golf.

Never just drop your rings in your pockets. You have tees and golf balls and a ball mark repair tool in there. It is too easy to lose them with all the shuffling around that happens during a round.

I remember a charity event I attended, and a new bride was in our group. As we gathered in the club house for dinner, she became frantic as she could not find either her wedding band or her engagement ring. We all searched the parking lot, her car trunk, the driving range and still no rings. I noticed the Pro Shop had closed, so I asked the manager to open it for us, just so we could take a quick peek around. By some miracle, they were there on the floor near a display she had admired earlier in the day. She was lucky and we were all very happy the story ended well. I gave her a little jewelry pouch when I saw her a few days later, but we never said a word to her husband. Like Vegas, what happens at the golf course stays at the golf course.

Imagine covering 18 holes looking for a diamond tennis bracelet and the odds of finding it. Best to store that precious gear before you warm up so you can enjoy it for years to come.

Lock your car and do not leave valuables in the front or back seat. Even private golf clubs get unwanted visitors who can quickly make your fun day turn to misery when you discover your car has been broken into and your laptop is gone. Lock your valuables in the trunk of your car or in your locker to be safe.

Extending the Invitation and Organizing the Day

When I invite a guest or guests, I give them a call several weeks, sometimes months, in advance so they can plan accordingly. I will ask if they prefer to walk or ride. A week or so before our outing, I will email the details of the day along with the name, address and phone number of my club. It's a good idea to give the club house or Pro Shop phone number in the event something comes up and they are delayed in traffic or have a last-minute emergency at home or work and must cancel. If I am somewhere in the club house on the day we play, and cannot take the call right away, I will at least get a message from the Pro Shop. Sometimes cell phone use is not allowed in the club house. File this under dotting the "I's" and crossing the "T's" as you do everything possible to make your day run smoothly.

In that confirming e-mail, I give a little biography of the group such as names, titles, companies, and handicaps of the other players in my group. If possible, I will add where they went to college or graduate school so everyone will have a chance to familiarize themselves with our foursome. I will mention the dress code and rules for cell phones in the invitation. I will also ask if everyone can stay on for lunch or dinner after the round.

Call the Pro Shop the day before you play to reconfirm your tee time and caddies if you requested them. Be prepared and you will never be blindsided.

Ask your guests to meet you in the Pro Shop at least forty-five minutes before you are scheduled to tee off. If you are hosting lunch before golf, suggest arrival time at least 90 minutes before tee time. That gives everyone time to get there, stop at the Bag Drop, change in the locker room if they are coming directly from the office, enjoy a brief lunch and have some time to warm up at the driving range before your tee time.

On the day you play, arrive about 20 minutes before your guests. Start with the Bag Drop and give the attendant $20. The names of your guests are on the tee sheet at the Bag Drop podium. Ask that your guests are told they do not have to give a gratuity. It has been covered. This is also a good time to tell the attendant how you want the golf carts loaded, especially if you are keen to ride with one guest in particular.

Once your group is ready to warm up, make sure there are scorecards, towels, pencils and water on the carts. Then you can head over to the Starter to confirm your group is checked in and you will be on the driving range. You will be called to the first tee a few minutes before your tee time comes up. Most groups need about 20-30 minutes to warm up. A little time at the range to loosen up and a little time on the practice green should give your guests an idea of how fast the greens are running that day.

This is a unique opportunity for you to further observe your guest/s and rely on your Business Golf IQ. Even their warm-up style can alert you as to how your day may unfold. Someone who just uses the driver is all about "drive for show". Play as quickly as possible and be ready for some competition. Someone who is more methodical will "putt for dough". This is the player you give all the details to, like wind, yardage, extra carry required on a hole and how the green breaks. The guest who is taking her time, looking around and drinking in the scenery could be there to relax and commune with nature. Golf is very social for her. Take your time and enjoy the day but remember the pace of play.

This warm-up period is also a good time to stroke the cards if you have agreed on any fun games you want to play, like a Nassau. Once you are at the first tee, take a moment to tell your guests a little bit about the hole such as the location of Penalty Areas or Bunkers, so they benefit from your local knowledge. Repeat this overview at the beginning of each hole. For example, you might say, "This is a sharp dogleg right, with three bunkers at the front of the green. There's water on the right, so you'll want to stay left side of the fairway."

If it is possible, ask the Starter to take a few pictures of your group with your phone so you can send them the next day via e-mail, but please do not post on social media. This friendly gesture of sending a group photo gives you another opportunity to get in front of your customer.

Tips about playing with caddies

There are those who could not even dream of a round without a caddy, while others are inveterate cart riders. Playing with an experienced caddy can be an uplifting experience. Much entertaining fiction and some hilarious true accounts have been written about the role of the caddy in golf's history books. I am not referring to some of the youngsters who make us feel we should be carrying our own bags by the 11th hole, but rather the men and women who have refined their skills and take great pride not only in their work but in how well you play under their guidance. Speaking of carrying a golf bag, you should own a light "stand and carry" bag. These bags have a stand that opens when the bag is put on the ground, keeping the bag upright, which allows easy access to your clubs. Think of it like a kickstand on a bicycle. Leave those big cart bags to the Professionals. Your caddy will thank you.

To ensure a good experience when you opt to walk with a caddy, follow these guidelines:

1)   Ask for an "A" caddy. You are paying for someone to help track your shots, rake bunkers, clean clubs, tend to the pin, replace divots, and offer strategic advice based on knowledge of the course, the playing conditions and the undulation of the greens. It doesn't take a good caddy long to size you up as a player and to make your round as successful and carefree as possible.

2)   You do not always have to take the advice of your caddy, especially if you like to read your own greens. However, if you do not know the course, my advice is to ask for an opinion *and* a read. Remember, you are paying for more than a bag carrier. You are renting local knowledge and years of experience.

3)   Let your caddy put the golf bag down before you grab a club. Better yet, just ask for the club you want. Don't feel bad about handing your club back once you have taken your shot. A good caddy will clean the club face and put it back in your bag. If you take a divot, the caddy replaces or fills it.

4)   It is your responsibility to buy your caddy food, snacks and beverages at the snack shack or from the beverage cart. On a hot day, your caddy will need even more water than you do. Especially if he or she is carrying two golf bags.

5)   At the end of the round, your caddy will clean your clubs, account for all 14 of them and either take them to the cart barn for storage if you are a private club member or take them to your car trunk if you are a guest. Ask your guests to check their bags to ensure all of their clubs are there, as well. On more than one occasion, despite the best efforts of the caddy, one of my clubs ended up in another player's bag or vice versa, especially if you

have the same set of clubs. You don't want to discover that error the next time you play and reach for your beloved 7-iron. Get some labels made for your golf clubs. These "stickers" wrap around your club just under the grip. Have your name and phone number on the labels. These labels can ensure a club left behind on a hole will find its way home to you.

You are the ATM for the Day

Be sure you have a good supply of singles, fives, tens and twenties to tip the various staff members who will help you with your day. Bag drop staff, locker room attendants, beverage cart drivers, snack shack and wait staff should all be recognized. If you take a caddy, plan on tipping in addition to the carry charge. Check with the Pro Shop to get the rates and their recommendations on tipping. Get all of this done well before your guests arrive so you are not scurrying about when you should be in the Pro Shop waiting for your guests. You want to be there to greet them and give them your undivided attention.

Should You Discuss Business?

If your guest asks you a specific question about your product or service, then of course you should engage. Some guests will ask many questions, others may simply want to play. Your time on the golf course is primarily to get to know people, for them to have a chance to come to know you better and to have fun. Your Business Golf IQ has put you with the decision maker, so try to be patient. If you want to introduce business into the conversation, do so only after at least four holes have been completed. Start your round with a general conversation. Nothing too heavy. Family, weather, sports, or the condition of the course are all quite neutral. Let the last three or four holes unfold as they may. If it is quiet, let it go. You still have the 19th hole. If your guest is opening up about what she needs or wants for her company, then by all means give the subject as much attention as necessary to build your relationship. The worst thing you can do is take the initiative and launch into an unsolicited pitch about how great your company is and what you can do for them. You need to first find out what they need. You won't hear very much if you do all the talking. Remember, these people have agreed to spend four hours of their time with you on the course, and some time with you after the round. Don't hold them hostage. Don't make or take cell phone calls or be sending texts while you are playing. It is distracting and considered to be quite rude. Business golf is a skill that requires patience and a sense of timing. Be an *active* listener and understand that not every round of golf seals the deal. Be prepared to have to spend more time building your relationship. It is a process and until you have earned their trust, you will need to continue to work on earning their business.

Letting Others Play Through

If you are enjoying a leisurely but steady pace with your foursome and a twosome is pushing you from behind, let them play through. While it is true that a twosome has no standing on the course, you are using good judgment by letting them go ahead of you. If you are walking with your guests and there's a foursome in motorized carts pushing behind you, let them through, assuming you are not waiting for a group ahead of you. If you have to let more than one group through, you are playing too slowly and you should pick up the pace. A good way to measure your pace of play is to complete the front nine in two hours. I am reminded of a sign that is posted at one of Boston's tonier private golf clubs. It reads, "It is the duty of every golfer to be just behind the group ahead, not directly ahead of the group behind." The reality is, unless your guest or guests are seasoned players, they may well struggle with the course and have some difficult holes that eat up time during a round. That is why you need to "vet" your guests beforehand and determine how to organize the day. If you are hosting them at your private club, you might want to consider what time to tee off and avoid the high-demand times. If your round is getting out of hand in terms of poor play, shift gears and suggest a scramble. It could well take the pressure off everyone and lighten up an otherwise disastrous outing.

At the Turn

"The Turn" is the expression used when golfers have finished the first nine holes, (the front nine), and are moving on to the 10th hole to begin the back nine, which will conclude on the 18th green. At the majority of 18-hole courses, there will be a snack shack and restrooms at the turn. Most golfers take a short break after nine holes to get something to eat and take it to the cart, make a quick visit to the restroom, and move on with as much speed as humanly possible. In other words, the turn is not the place for a sit-down luncheon. It is more like a "grab and go" and shouldn't take more than five minutes. As host for the day, you are responsible for the tab and the tip, and to keep everyone moving. You can help speed things up if there is a number to call for the "Shack" so you can place your order with the attendant when you reach the 9th hole tee box. That certainly would help with the pace of play for any club that uses this system.

Nutrition and Hydration Impacts Your Game

During the round, it's important to keep your body hydrated. Drinking plenty of water or a sports drink with electrolytes during a round on a hot summer day, even if you don't feel thirsty, will keep you mentally sharp and your muscles happy and relaxed. In extremely hot weather, by the time you feel thirsty, you are already dehydrated. Snacks such as bananas, apples, grapes, nuts and dried fruit give you energy, but won't drag you down like candy or other sweets, which gives a quick sugar high but then a sharp energy drop about 30 minutes later.

If you are playing early in the morning, a good breakfast will keep you going until lunch. If you are playing in the afternoon, try some protein and a salad before you tee off. The goal is to keep your energy level even all day so you can feel and play your best.

Should I Let My Guests Win?

Absolutely not! As Susan Bond-Philo, PGA says, "Never back down. I've played with men all my life and have had many playing interviews which resulted in me playing some of my best golf ever."

The thing to remember here is to play your best every time you play. The longer you play golf, the more you will realize that we all have bad days or a few bad shots on the course. People who love and respect this great game all know that an occasional bad shot or even a bad round is as much a part of golf as the grass you stand on. But it is simply not right to throw your game because your guest is having a bad day, or because he or she has a higher rank than you do in the corporate pecking order. Be admired because you are a good player, not because you are willing to capitulate.

The Nineteenth Hole: Making the Most of Post-Round Time

At the end of the round, be sure to thank everyone for coming and shake hands on the 18th green. Make sure your guests' clubs have been taken to their cars and invite them to freshen up in the Locker Room. It's time to head to the 19th hole, which is usually the bar or the grille room. Better yet, if there is a lovely outside area to sit and relax, it may afford more privacy and make it easier to discuss a little business.

Some clubs do not allow hats, visors, cell phone use or smoking once inside, so please advise your guests accordingly. That is why including this information in the e-mail you sent confirming the date takes the pressure off you to enforce the rules.

Sometimes, a guest will just want to head home if he or she is a bit more introverted. Do not be upset or alarmed. Just thank them for coming and tell them you will give them a call next week to set up a time to meet. (Your 19th hole.) This is a rare occurrence, but I just don't want you to be surprised or disappointed should this happen. I know a player who is a single-digit handicapper and one of the nicest ladies you could ever meet. She has yet to come inside for a drink after a round of golf. That is her way and we do not judge her for her choice. I am not trying to earn her business or paying for her round, so she can do as she pleases.

When you get settled at a table, keep in mind that you are hosting clients or potential clients. While a cold beer or cocktail can be quite refreshing after a round, don't get carried away by having too much to drink. Your body has lost a good deal of water through perspiration and physical exertion during the last several hours. Any alcohol that enters your system will be soaked up into your bloodstream like a dry sponge absorbing water. Maybe one of your guests doesn't drink alcohol. When someone from the waitstaff comes to your table you can begin with, "May we have four glasses of ice water to start?" Once the water is delivered to your table, you can then follow up with, "May I get you something else cold to drink? Would you care for some iced tea, soda or another beverage?" That keeps the situation light and doesn't put pressure on anyone.

By beginning with water all around, your guests have the option of taking their own next step from there. If someone wants the ubiquitous cold beer or a gin and tonic, and you want to join them, you should just have one and switch back to something soft. Sparkling water with a wedge of lime looks just like a cocktail but doesn't give the kick. The bottom line here is that this post-round time is for making the final good impression for the day. If you've played well out on the course and have gained the respect and admiration of your colleagues or prospective clients, but end up tipsy because you had a little too much to drink, then you have lost at the game of business golf. You have lost some of that ever-important personal currency, no matter how low your score was for the day.

Golf, like boating, is a boozy culture. It is way too easy to get caught up in the laughter and joviality at the yacht club or golf club. It isn't until that wave of intoxication rolls over you that you realize you're smashed. I am not preaching here but simply giving you the benefit of over 30 years of participation in and observation of people at private clubs and a decade of boating with my husband. I have seen a good many golfers stumble into an Uber while their cars stay the night in the club parking lot. Cha-ching. More personal currency down the drain. It is too easy for an onlooker to wonder if you are sloppy at the bar, are you sloppy with your business?

With your clear head, use this time to see if your guests who are prospective clients have any questions about your products or services. If not, wait a few days or a week and call to schedule a meeting. Then you can try to move closer to closing a deal on what then becomes the 20th hole. Closing a deal doesn't always happen right away, unless you are meeting an immediate need or solving a serious problem. Good relationships anchored in trust and mutual respect take time to build, but once established, rarely fade. If your guests are current clients, use the time to tell them how much you appreciate their business. This is a good time to offer a gift be it a hat with your club logo, a box of golf balls, or whatever you feel best suits the occasion. This smooth gesture is their cue that the outing is concluded and it is time for everyone to leave when you leave. Don't stretch out post-round time until the wee hours. You are a busy, successful person with a demanding schedule and a balanced life.

Send a text or e-mail the next day telling them it was a pleasure to host them. If you have a good group picture from the first tee, you can attach it. As mentioned earlier, do not post on any social media.

Once you close the deal, you will want to document your success so your boss will see your golf expenditures are well worth the money and the time, and will solidify you as a rainmaker.

The more you host colleagues and clients, the easier this whole routine becomes. Ask some of your friends who do this regularly how they arrange the day. With time and a little experience, you will become a *power golfer*.

"The little ball just sits there until you make it go somewhere else. In that regard, golf is very much like life itself: It awaits your intention and action before revealing the mysteries of the outcome."

The Big Leap: Conquer Your Hidden Fear and Take Life to the Next Level by Guy Hendricks

Chapter 4

Charity and Private Club Golf Outings
How to be a Great Host or Guest

Golf: The Springboard for Your Success

The female executive who is willing to take her business acumen onto the golf course and use golf as a business tool can begin by following announcements of charity and corporate golf outings in the local newspapers and association newsletters. Thousands of businesses, nonprofit organizations, healthcare providers, manufacturers of consumer goods, retailers, financial institutions and other service providers lend their names to golf outings every year.

Because of golf's long-standing reputation as a game of honor coupled with unfailing traditions like good sportsmanship and integrity, it makes sense for companies to align their brands with golf. "Good corporate citizenship" was a phrase my former boss at BankBoston used many times over the years. Whether we were working with The World Affairs Council, The Japan Society, The Consular Corps in Boston, or taking the members of the Bank's Board of Directors to visit our offices in 33 countries around the globe, the bank understood that businesses, whether large or small, have to maintain a visible presence and be active in the communities they serve. When it comes to charity golf outings, these good corporate citizens are often willing to offer support.

For many of the C-Suite Executives and successful Entrepreneurs I know from my clubs, membership in a private club is often part of their compensation package. They have a good sense of what charity and corporate golf outings do to enhance corporate branding and solidify their image as industry leaders. In some instances, someone might help with booking that coveted Monday afternoon spot during a summer prime-time month to help with the first step in making your golf event a success. What is the first step? Location, location, location. Where you host your event, especially if is at an upscale private golf club, will make people want to participate and support the effort.

Promoting Your Company

There are many ways to position yourself and your company successfully in a charity or corporate golf outing. These events are the result of months of hard work from the planning committee. Tasks like recruiting foursomes and selling ads for the program book are delegated by the Chair. Retaining sponsors, securing special prizes for the hole-in-one contest, longest drive, and closest to the pin are high on the priority list. Determining the awards for low gross and low net winners is another task to be managed. Planning the menu, soliciting raffle prizes, getting high-end silent auction donations, like a round for 4 to play Pinnacle at Troon North, in Scottsdale, Arizona and collecting tee gift donations for the welcome bags are yet more details that need to be delegated and managed. The bottom line is to meet or surpass the fundraising goals the charity has established. If you are a beginning golfer, and not quite ready to play in a golf event, volunteer to serve on the planning committee or help out on the day of the event. Just from attending meetings and recruiting sponsors and players, the networking alone will help you to meet new people. It is an easy way to enter the world of business golf until you feel ready to play.

If you own a small business and plan to play in the event, invite three of your best customers to make up your foursome. If you are a senior executive within a large corporation, consider organizing a few foursomes. Ask your top executive golfers to host three of their best clients. The business golf world is all about exposure, networking and following up on (and closing) new business opportunities. It is also a highly effective way to maintain solid relationships with existing clients.

Signage is a big part of any charity or corporate golf outing. You can get your company name printed on little things like tees or your logo printed on the gift bags. For a small investment and a bit of your time, offer to host a round of golf for three at your private golf club. Work with an auto dealer to arrange for that spiffy new SUV to be on display for a Par 3 hole-in-one contest. Auto dealers do this often, in fact, they carry insurance for it, but only when your event has the right audience. In other words, if you are working on the Children's Hospital Oncology Unit Annual Charity Golf Outing, and it sells out every year at the most sought after club around, you will find it easy to meet your goals. But if you are working on a small event like raising money for the Junior High Girls Golf Team, don't expect that level of support. Better to book a good public course with a dining facility and look to local businesses for support. (Don't look down on the public courses. Some of them are the finest tracks in the world. Pebble Beach and Pinehurst #2 are perfect examples.) Golf outings are expensive because you are paying for green fees, golf carts and food/beverage service before you even put a tee in the ground. Another piece of advice is not to expect a private club to lower their fees for your event. Yours is just one of the many Monday Outside Outings they have on their books for worthy causes who rent the facilities at that club year after year.

The most important point here is if you raise your hand to volunteer, make sure you follow through and deliver the goods. Nothing will make you look worse than talking a good game and then doing nothing to help. Your name will not be on the roster next year. There we go with "personal currency" again, and a few more of your valuable coins have been lost. Implied in being a member of this planning committee is the notion that you will recruit *several* foursomes, secure advertising in the program book, and solicit great prizes. You must be prepared not only to make a commitment with your time but to spend some of your money when you play in a charity event.

For a modest investment, your company could underwrite the box lunch or be the beverage cart sponsor in exchange for recognition in the program book and signage on the beverage cart. Consider other promotional materials like tee signs. Sponsoring a hole will get your company name and logo on a sign that is displayed on that hole for the entire day. Every player will see it. Have a sign professionally made and take it with you to use in other golf events your company sponsors. Donate a prize for the raffle or auction, which also gets your name in the printed program. A case of wine, a Spa Day, or a gift certificate at a popular restaurant are all good items to donate. Many companies have tees, visors, baseball hats, or golf towels made up with the company's name and logo to donate to the welcome bags handed out at the registration table. There are dozens of price points and opportunities to promote yourself and your company at charity outings. Decide which level of participation suits your goals and budget, then proceed with gusto.

A well-run outing leaves a great impression on the participants. These events demand outstanding planning, superb management on the day of the event, and plenty of volunteers who have their roles clearly explained and properly managed throughout the day. If you have ever been to a US Open or a Ryder Cup event, they run like a cruise ship the day she returns to port. The mission is clear, thousands disembark, cabins are cleaned, new linens put down, the galley is restocked and the ship is polished from stem to stern. Every employee on the ship knows the vessel must be sparkling and ready to sail in just a few hours, before thousands more embark on their dream cruise. Even minute details like returning a well-loved Teddy Bear, left behind in the cabin, to a distraught toddler are all considered to be part of the excellent service.

I went to the Ryder Cup in 1999 and US Open in 2022. Both events were held at The Country Club in Brookline, Massachusetts. I was thoroughly impressed with how thousands of Event Pass Holders were greeted by event volunteers stationed at the reserved public parking lots and garages. We did not have to wonder where to go the moment we entered the parking area. The experience started before we even parked the car. (Or pahked the cah if you're from Boston.) We were guided to board waiting executive motor coaches and deposited at the Main Gate. The hospitality tents were outstanding, the merchandise tent was crowded and well-stocked, and yet it only took a few minutes to check out. All around me was a sense of tranquility and orderliness, but orchestrating the event took thousands of hours of planning, anticipating customer needs and committing to exceeding their expectations.

Many companies today host their own corporate outings and invite customers and prospects out to a great private club for an afternoon of golf, followed by dinner. Again, there are dozens of details that, if not properly executed, will do your brand more harm than good. Get your special events people involved or hire a professional golf outing management company to make your day of golf a memorable success. They will be there for you from the first planning meeting, designing and getting the invitations out, ironing out all the glitches during the hectic weeks before your event and on duty the day of the event to make sure everything you have planned over the previous months is all executed professionally and without a hitch. They will even have a "post-event" meeting to review the event and discuss where things might be expanded, streamlined, or improved for next year's event.

Don't be afraid to dream big. Have you noticed that beautiful gold **Rolex** logo we see over the scoreboard during the exciting LPGA and PGA events? Golf and corporate branding are intertwined. Look at the advertisers you see during a televised golf event touting luxury cars, cruises, high-end timepieces, private jet services and a host of financial services. The desire for successful people to be associated with excellent products and services will not be changing anytime soon. Most recently, brands that sponsor the LPGA are found to have gained up to 400% return on their investment, according to a report from SponsorUnited. Businesses have long known that golf enjoys a sterling reputation based on honor and integrity. Companies who support golf want to present themselves as good corporate citizens who also share the values of the game of golf. They want to demonstrate their trustworthiness to golf's affluent audience and gain them as customers.

What to Expect When You Play in or Host a Charity or Corporate Golf Event

Now that you have some of the "Why" of business golf, let's examine the "How". When you play in a golf event, here is a rundown of how a day might unfold. To host, put a foursome together and vary playing abilities to make it an easy day for a newer golfer. Invite a "better player" who is a good sport to carry the team a bit. Remember to use your Business Golf IQ to put a compatible team together. Do your homework on handicaps and personalities and you will ensure a memorable day. Suggest your guests arrive at least 60 minutes before the scheduled starting time. Confirm all details in an e-mail or phone call the day before.

There are always quite a few things to do before you actually tee off. Your most important job as the host is to have a **large supply of cash** with you. Singles, fives, tens, twenties and even a few $100s will come in handy and save you from the embarrassment of being unprepared. I know we all use Credit and Debit Cards, Apple Pay, Venmo and so on, but when hosting a group in a charity outing, Cash is King.

Let's begin as you drive up to the Bag Drop, where your clubs will be removed from your trunk. You'll be told your starting hole. Tip that person $20 and tell him you are covering for your guests.

Those guys have a roster with all groups, player names and starting holes. Get your vehicle parked and your golf shoes on. Your first stop will be the Registration Table where you will check in and receive a welcome bag filled with goodies. There will also be a program book outlining the day's events, the list of prizes and contest holes as well as ads from the event sponsors and supporters. If this event is selling Mulligans, and you are the host, you should buy them all for your group. Ask the Registration Table staff to tell your guests that Mulligans (a chance to take a shot over) have been purchased when they arrive and check in. Mulligans, you will soon find, are excellent to use on the green if someone just missed a birdie putt.

You will probably get another reminder of your starting hole. No tip for the volunteers seated here, but be prepared for an onslaught of volunteers asking you to buy Raffle Tickets. Prices vary but don't skimp and buy a few for your guests. Raffle tickets are usually something like 10 for $20, 50 for $100 or something along those lines. Mulligans are usually a nominal amount. Just remember it all goes to the Charity.

If you are at a private club Guest Day, there may be a Skins challenge with a large pot of cash at the end of the day for the lucky winner. Maybe the winner will buy her group a round of drinks before she heads to the Pro Shop to spend her earnings.

In Charity outings, I have seen almost every cash pot returned to the Charity by the kind-hearted winner. That speaks volumes about how to build personal currency. It is a gesture that will be noticed by many and appreciated by the Charity.

Private club guest days are quite another story. Your welcome bag might contain a sleeve of or even a dozen golf balls, a golf umbrella, a golf towel or a hat or visor, all bearing the logo of the club where you are playing. There may be golf shirts or wind shirts or golf shoes arranged by size on several tables where you can make your choices. Everything here is budget-driven, so if you paid a Mercedes-Benz entrance fee, expect to be wowed. If the Registration Form you completed asks for shirt or shoe sizes, then there will be tables set up and staffed where you and your guests can collect those gifts. One guest day I attended, Maui Jim sunglasses set up a table with their staff there to help you select the pair you like. I have to say, they are spectacular sunglasses whether you golf, ski, boat or just walk the dog. But I digress. Can you tell I just love getting wonderful welcome goodies?

If you are a guest at a private club golf event, it is incumbent upon you to bring a very nice gift for your host. You can give it before or after the round.

After you have checked in at a Charity outing, make your way into the club house and find the restroom to freshen up. If there is a buffet lunch, you can fuel up before you head to the cart staging area. Most likely, you will have meet up with your guests or host either at the registration table or at the lunch table. Sometimes, rather than lunch inside, an outing will offer box lunches on the golf carts. Again, these decisions are all budget-driven.

Whether this is a Charity or Guest Day outing, the golf carts, with all the players' bags loaded, will be lined up at the driving range. Carts will have players' names and starting holes, so it is easy to find your cart. Drop your gift bag in the basket on the cart, grab a few clubs and head to the practice area to warm up and roll a few putts. Your scorecard with the appropriate strokes for your foursome will be on the steering wheel along with any special instructions for the day.

About 10 minutes before your shotgun start, it is helpful to the club staff if you head over to your cart. You can chat with your group and say hello to the folks in nearby carts (always be networking) and get your gear squared away. Shortly, there will be a welcome announcement from the Head Golf Professional over the PA system. You will be informed of any local rules, contest holes, the importance of replacing divots and repairing ball marks on the greens and how long your round should take.

In a Charity outing, employees of the club will be in golf carts, ready to assist all players to their starting holes, so don't worry about getting lost. Once all players have reached their starting holes, a horn will sound signaling all players to tee off. There will be signs directing you to every hole and restroom on the course, so no worries there either.

As you make your way around the course during a Charity outing, the real hawking begins. The outing volunteers are stationed on many holes and will be offering you more raffle tickets and perhaps a hit the green/double your money contest. The good sports who hit the green and win will just give it back to the charity. There may be a hole where you can "hire" the Pro to hit your drive for a modest donation, which again, goes to the Charity. Now you see why you need to stop at the ATM when you play in Charity events and carry the cash with you. You also will have the Beverage Cart driving around, and that person always appreciates a tip when you buy cold drinks or snacks for your guests.

In a private club Guest Day, things are a little different. You might have food set up out on the course with the chef and club staff members offering an array of delicious food and beverages. There may be holes that offer a taste of single malt scotch, or a neck massage chair available while you wait to hit on a busy Par 3.

I can tell you, Charity, Corporate or Guest Day, these are fun outings, but long days. Most golf outings, Charity or Corporate, will most likely take five or more hours, quite a bit more than the usual four hours expected from players. So please remember to drink lots of water and wear sunscreen, but most of all just have fun. You are a team, so no need to stress out. Honestly, it's not about winning, it's about the time you are spending with your clients and creating the unique relationship that only a round of golf can provide.

After the Round

You will be able to take the golf cart to your car so you can put your clubs in the trunk. Depending on the club and its facilities, along with the tone of the event, some players might like to change into a clean shirt after the round, especially on a hot and humid day. These events do not require a change of clothes, so perhaps just a trip to the locker room or ladies' room to freshen up is certainly sufficient.

If you are hosting a group for the Charity outing, meet your guests at the bar where you will buy the refreshments and head to the Silent Auction table. Be prepared for another offer or two to buy more raffle tickets. Then you can go to your assigned dinner table with your guests. The dining area is usually set with tables of 8, so you will have an opportunity to meet some new folks and talk about your day on the course during dinner. Along with cash, you will need to have your business cards with you.

If you have not had the opportunity to talk a little business out on the course, use this time for casual business conversation and further relationship building. If you know other people who are there, be sure to introduce your guests. Quite often people will know each other from college or previous business dealings. It is always appreciated if you can facilitate expanding someone's network that leads to business. That certainly contributes to your personal currency. But first, getting your own deal done is your priority. The same advice holds true when you are a private club guest or host.

It's a good idea not to linger after dinner and the awards. It's also a good idea not to have too much to drink. Remember, whether you are the host or the guest, you are representing your company and who you are as a professional. End the day with the respect and admiration of your guests or host. I know, there I go again about personal currency. But rest assured, people take notice of things you do when you are at events like this. The player who professionally conducts herself might just be getting a call to talk about her product or service from someone who watched how she conducted herself apres-golf. Perhaps even a new job offer could come from someone who attended the event and noticed how she handled herself on the range with her guests. Confidence and class always make a lasting impression whether you are the host or the guest. This is how you *drive your business to success.*

Be sure to thank your guests for coming or your host for inviting you and send a text or email the next day saying how much you enjoyed their company and hope that they had a good time. Set up a time to meet to discuss your proposal for them or to find out more about how you might help them with their business. Never be afraid to ask for someone's business when you feel the time is right.

"On the golf course, concentrate on the present, forget the past and don't look too far ahead."

Judy Rankin

Chapter 5

Strengthen Your Mind and Body

Think Your Way to Better Golf

Mind and Body. Body and mind. Just as the rules and etiquette of golf are intertwined, the same is true for the mental side of our game. How we *think* about what we do can actually help our bodies to perform better.

At one of the meetings I arranged for the members of my Boston-area Business and Professional Women's Golf Association, a personal fitness trainer came to speak with us about exercises to do over the winter months to stay fit for golf. She also shared some insight into the minds of the Olympic athletes she had helped to train over the years.

The speaker, Cathy Von Klemperer, shared this with us, "Positive thinking is a key to self-confidence. Unlike physical skills, it is a mental skill that can be observed only by you. You must be aware of what you think and say to yourself when you practice and play. Ask yourself if you are thinking about your skills or if you are doubting yourself. Remember this, winners think about what they *want* to happen, and losers think about what they fear *might* happen. You must use your thoughts to direct your attention and behavior." Cathy had our undivided attention. She then introduced one of her clients, a young mother of three, who had just finished another road race that September weekend. "I never was an athlete," she began softly. "I thought having asthma meant I couldn't run. That was three months ago. Since I started working with Cathy, I run three miles, four times a week and have entered many two-mile road races. I feel more confident, adventurous and proactive in all areas of my life."

Making My Own Commitment

It took me a few weeks of thinking about all the things Cathy and her client had said to us at that meeting before I finally picked up the phone and asked for an appointment.

"I want to be a better golfer," I told her. "I'm taking lessons, I'm practicing and playing, but I'm not building more strength and I'm not training my mind to *think* about being a better golfer."

Cathy suggested a time. In fact, she suggested six times. Once a week for six weeks. I was going to brain boot camp.

The first visit was spent talking about my business, my schedule, and what other sports I enjoyed like tennis, skiing, biking, and walking. We talked about the power of meditation, the benefits of daily stretching, and some athletic goals we could set for a six-week period, to be followed by goals for a six-month period. She gave me some reading to do on the benefits of meditation, some stretches to incorporate into my day, and suggested I come the following week in workout clothes. She also gave me a daily log to fill out each time I completed an activity: stretch, golf, bike and so on. That is why I would encourage all golfers to keep a journal. It helps us to see, and prove positively, the time and effort we have made to become better golfers. Sometimes an extended business trip, a sick child or parent, or the pressure of preparing for a conference or major presentation, will require us to put golf aside for a week or two. Keeping a journal will remind us of how much we have accomplished and encourages us to stay with it.

Each time I meditated, I told myself I had a smooth golf swing, along with other positive affirmations for the week. Each time I rode my bike 10 miles, I could feel my legs getting stronger. In a very short period of time, I had totaled 150 miles. Then I tried a 15-mile ride and on it went. It was mentally exhilarating and spiritually empowering.

When I went to play golf, I did some warm-up stretches at home. Before I got on the first tee, I would do a brief deep breathing exercise and mentally tell myself, "I am a good golfer. I have a smooth swing". Then, I would picture my friend Susan Bond-Philo's easy yet powerful swing in my mind's eye. Let me tell you, it worked. Not every time, but enough to make me believe you *can* think your way to achievement in sports and in business. My handicap started going down, my golf association membership was going up.

Mind over Muscles?

Much research has been conducted over the years on the correlation between mentally rehearsing a technique or movement and how it translates into enhanced physical ability. It seems that swinging a club in mental practice turns on some of the brain circuits used when a player swings for real on the golf course.

That is why a practice swing can be so helpful during your round of golf, especially when you are starting out. You are engaging your mind to tell your body that you will be requiring a particular movement in just a moment. You are "envisioning" the shot you want to make and the outcome you want to realize.

Combined with lessons, regular practice and frequent play, you will build muscle memory and increase self-confidence over time.

Golf Exercises

Decades ago when most people thought about golf, they did not necessarily think about fitness, especially when we see some players riding about in motorized golf carts while sipping a cold beer or any icy High Noon. While golf is more a skill sport than an endurance sport like swimming, tennis, or running a marathon, it still requires muscles to be in good shape and loose for optimum performance.

Since most of the power in a golf swing comes from a strong core and leg muscles, exercises that build strength in these areas are the key to power and distance. Building strength in your arms will also contribute to a better game. Brisk walking, cycling and weight training are all great ways to tone muscles and build strength. Tennis, swimming, and rowing will give additional upper body strength and expand your aerobic capacity. I still ride my bike, swim and walk, and I love a session on the Elliptical or rowing machine.

Whatever you enjoy that keeps you moving, embrace some form of physical activity on a regular basis.

Hydration

Somehow, there is a biological disconnect between the mind and the body when it comes to thirst. We know when we're hungry and we know when we are sick, cold or injured, but by the time we "feel" thirsty on the golf course, the horse has left the barn, and we are dehydrated.

Our bodies are loaded with water. Somewhere between 40 to 50 quarts. Yet losing even a tiny bit of your body water, say 2%, will have a negative impact on your game. You may experience a dip in concentration, feel fatigued, or even have a muscle cramp if you are not properly hydrated. This can happen as soon as just one hour into your round, especially on a hot day.

For top performance, drink at least one glass of water before teeing off and try to drink at least half a cup of water or a sports drink after every hole. The sports drink (like Gatorade) has electrolytes that keep you better hydrated. Increase this intake if the weather is hot and humid. Have a tall glass of water after your round.

Learn Course Management

Course management is as much a part of your golf training as putting and chipping practice is to developing your finesse around the greens.

And what exactly is course management? Suppose you have a shot off the tee that slices to the right and comes to rest on the adjacent fairway. The ball lands at the beginning of a stand of trees that divides the two fairways and is about 75 yards in length. You can see your ball and your mind starts to churn as you get closer. Upon reaching your ball, here is how the situation looks. Ahead of you, there's a narrow opening in the trees that a perfect 4-iron shot could get through. Let's call this Option 1. Or maybe you could lob the ball over the trees with a perfect 9-iron shot and advance the ball that way. This will be Option 2. Let's consider a third option. Would you elect to laterally "punch" the ball out with a hooded 5-iron and get it back into play with a 90% success rate vs a 10% success rate? Are Options 1 and 2 shots you practice all the time? Ask yourself if you feel confident standing over those shots.

In golf, as in business, we need to get back on track as soon as possible after a minor setback. We don't want to try something risky that could cost us profit in business or additional strokes on our scorecard. In golf, we often have to manage the situation to keep an unfortunate event from becoming a disaster. Sometimes, frankly, we need to go sideways in order to move forward.

Let's play out a possible scenario for each option so you can see exactly why sound course management is so critically important to becoming a better golfer.

Note that I've used the word "perfect" in the first two options for a reason. As amateur golfers, we occasionally hit a *perfect* shot. Bully for us and that is what keeps us coming back. The Golf

Professionals, on the other hand, occasionally hit a *bad* shot. That's why they work on their game for hours every day.

Option 1) Suppose your 4-iron shot hits a tree and bounces right back at you. In fact, it flies past you by about 50 yards. Now you've *lost* yardage and added at least another stroke to get back into play and are no closer to the green.

Option 2) Suppose your 9-iron lob over the trees is hit fat or not high enough and now you're *in* the trees. Add at least another stroke to get out from under the branches and back onto your fairway. Oh, and don't forget you cannot build a stance by bending or breaking limbs and branches. If you do, it's a two-stroke penalty.

Now, let's look at what good course management will do for you.

Option 3) Gently "punch" your shot out with a low iron (5- or 6-iron) and the ball will roll onto the middle of your fairway. You'll be able to see the green and you could be on the green or at least close to it with your third shot. Being in the middle of *your* fairway and seeing *your* target will give you confidence and a real opportunity to execute a good third shot and save those extra strokes.

I share this with you, my friends, from my own experiences as a new golfer trying to execute Options 1 or 2. Yeah, that tree branch 2-stroke penalty as well. It is all in the learning process and the humbling experiences that time spent playing golf will teach you. Hopefully, this story will help you someday if you find yourself in a similar predicament. I hope you don't, but now you are prepared.

Keeping our minds focused and under control is one of the most important parts of our golf game. Can we teach ourselves to think about the next shot and forgive ourselves for the bad one? It's easy, after three or four bad shots in a row, to start saying, "I'm a lousy player. I can't do this." Try giving yourself a mental mulligan and switch your mind from negative self-talk to something more positive. There is no "perfect" in golf. All we can do is keep trying, so don't sell those clubs yet.

I had a terrific phone conversation recently with Kathy Hart Wood, LPGA. Her coaching company, **Above Par**, is about "Golf and the Mind". She teaches and lectures all over the country and works with both individuals and companies to delve into "what's on your mind" when you play golf. All without watching you hit a single golf ball. Kathy has been "behind the ropes" as a competitor, worked as a golf instructor and was Head of Women's Golf. She is recognized as one of the top 50 golf teachers in the country and is one of the most open and amusing ladies you could ever meet. You can follow her on LinkedIn, watch her on YouTube or visit her at KathyHartWood.com. You can also download her new podcast, *Above Par,* on Amazon.

One of things we talked about was how to "exorcise" a really bad hole from your memory. Considering the old adage that golf is "played in the 6 inches between your ears", here is what Kathy believes is a way to replace a bad memory with a good one.

1) After your round, go back to the driving range, putting green, or practice bunker and hit the shot that caused you the problem out on the course. Just 10 minutes might be all you need to feel a little better, to rebuild your confidence and end your day on a happy note.

2) Try to remain Neutral about your score. A number is just a number. It is neutral. It only takes on meaning when you assign a meaning to it. Are you judging yourself by a certain number or are you feeling that others are judging you? I laughed out loud when she said some people are upset when asked "How was your game today?" It might be interpreted by the golfer who had a lousy day as akin to asking any woman walking down the street, "Hey, how much do you weigh?" On the other hand, if you just shot your best

round ever, be it 72 or 122, you are going to be happy. If you usually shoot 95 and shoot 115, you might not be as perky. So try to see your score as just a number and not a judgment on you or your ability.

3) Ask yourself what you might have done differently on that terrible hole. Perhaps change your strategy a bit. Consider a lay-up shot if you constantly find the bunker on the right from the tee box or end up in a penalty area, plunked in the water on the left. Consider using more or less club or choosing a different target. Whatever you need to do to change your outcome, give it a try the next time you play that hole. Kathy said, "We learn from our mistakes. A mistake is only a negative event if we allow ourselves to view it that way."

4) Every time you are on that hole, standing on the tee, your mind will bring up the vision of your bad experience on that hole. Our minds do that to protect us from our biologically ingrained flight or fight response. Suddenly, you are awash with adrenaline. Take a deep breath, see the bad thought and then let it float on by. It's time to make some new and better memories on that hole.

The 3 Cs: Calm, Confident and Certain

In one of her podcasts, Kathy Hart Wood offered some tremendous insights on anger. What are its roots, causes and outcomes? She explained that anger has four components: The Build Up, The Spark, The Explosion and The Aftermath.

We all want to play in a good frame of mind: calm, confident and certain are Kathy's favorite Cs. We might begin our day with these 3 Cs on our minds, but Kathy told me that your anger might well start building in your car on the way to play golf. Something might happen like a traffic jam, an argument with a partner or a snarky teenager. Perhaps a slow driver ahead of you caused you to worry about making your tee time.

We all know that something or some things are going to happen during a round of golf that will upset us. Someone might have been too loud at the practice range while you were trying to warm up. Maybe someone in your foursome was late for your tee time and it was irritating and distracting. Once you settled down on the tee, maybe your drive landed in a divot or went into a Penalty Area, so you did not get the score you expected to make on the first hole. Then someone in your group walked on your putt line on the second hole so you missed your putt for par, and then maybe someone else in your group was a little too chatty for your mood today. You try to tap your anger down but you are still saying to yourself, "Why does this always happen to me? This is just so unfair."

This, she says, is the "Build Up", the first step toward anger. Kathy maintains that there is nothing wrong with anger. It is a human emotion like joy, fear and sadness. As as we try to manage our 3 Cs, we need to learn how to manage anger, as well. "Anger," Kathy told me, "gives away our power. It is a terrible state to be in." Suddenly your grip tightens, you start swinging harder and faster, the double and triple bogies pile up and your game is in the tank.

If you have ever seen an old black and white TV cowboy show, the good guy always exclaims, just before the first punch is thrown, "That's the last straw, Podner!", and wham, the bad guy gets knocked out. Whatever that "last straw" is for the golfer whose anger is now bubbling over is called "The Spark".

Wait! What was *that*? Did you just throw a club? Kick the golf cart? Throw a golf ball into the pond? Launch a profanity-laced diatribe that now floats in the air over you like a dark cloud?

Well, *that* was "The Explosion". People around you are shocked, you are embarrassed. It is an awkward moment for everyone to say the least. You apologize for your outburst in what is finally "The Aftermath". The volcano erupted, the pot boiled over and onto the stove and now you need to clean up the mess. As one of my friends told me after she had a meltdown on the 15th hole, "I just wanted to walk into the water and disappear. I don't know what came over me. I just lost it." Well, my friend had just shot a nifty 42 on the front nine. However, the back nine was not going so well after a few doubles and a triple bogey dashed her hopes of an excellent round for the day. "I am so very sorry.", she said over and over.

So let's try to rewind the tape on this saga and give you some tools to help you manage anger on the golf course. "Number one," Kathy told me, "is to notice the anger. If it is just a small annoyance, can you put it in a bucket and let it go? What are you thinking or saying to yourself that is letting the anger build? Can you stop it? Can you give yourself a mental mulligan with a 30-second time out to cool down? Can you regulate whatever is in your mind and not let it show up in your body?"

This is perhaps a good time for a long drink of cold water and a snack. Maybe your blood sugar is low and you need a little energy. Ask yourself is the mental state you are in caused by someone in your foursome or something bothering you at work? These are external forces. Or are you upset with yourself and your negative self-talk as the internal force that's winding you up? Learning how to *see* your anger and to process it as just another emotion should hopefully get you back to Calm, Certain and Confident. Better yet, give Kathy Hart Wood a call to get your mind back in the game. Wouldn't she be a great speaker at your next corporate golf event?

We are just amateurs, so when we are having a lousy round, try not to be a poor sport and ruin the round for those folks playing – and paying – alongside you. Once again, it is just a game and we are supposed to be having fun. Things will get better, but only if you give yourself permission to be human and to relax.

Don't give up on golf, and try not to give in to negative self-talk, and most of all try not to get down on yourself. So what if you have to pick up on a hole? Get back on the tee at the next hole and whack it again. As Cathy Von Klemperer said, "Once we begin to train ourselves, to treat our thoughts and mental images as though they are subject to our control, we will begin to feel the power of mind over body."

In golf, we have to keep telling ourselves we can do this. We have to keep showing ourselves, through mental discipline, that good shots will follow a series of poor shots. If we stay *focused* and *think* about performing better, improvement will come.

Be kind to yourself. We have all done it. Told ourselves we stink, we are idiots, we can't believe we made such a stupid mistake and on it goes. Take a moment to consider how you might feel if someone in your foursome spoke to you in this manner. It would be hurtful and upsetting. No doubt, it would make you angry. Most likely, it would be the end of the friendship. So, tell yourself, it's just golf. Everyone has bad shots. What does it accomplish to berate yourself? Chin up, dust yourself off and go hit the ball again. Now that's a golfer who is calm, confident and certain.

I believe that winners, regardless of what the scorecard reads, are those who maintain their composure and are mindful that they are with friends or colleagues who should not have to endure a tirade. Winners are those who encourage a friend after she has had a bad hole. Winners will quickly and quietly rake the bunker for you after it took you three shots to get out and traveled only 5 yards.

I used to play with a lady at Copperleaf in Estero, FL and she always had a quip about a bad day of golf. About halfway through a lousy round, she would shrug her shoulders and say, "Guess it's time to put my happy face on." She played long enough, and well enough, to know that we aren't "on" every single round. She was a delight both on and off the course.

Be Decisive

"Get good at making decisions," Kathy Hart Wood tells her students. As you ride or walk to your shot, always be thinking about what club you are going to use, what your yardage is to the flag stick and what target line you are going to focus on. Being decisive is a good habit to develop. It builds confidence and it helps to speed play. There will be times, especially on blustery days when the wind is in your face, that you may opt to go down a club once you are standing over your ball. There is nothing wrong with that, but please do not make a habit of going back and forth to your bag, three or four times, while others are waiting for their turn to hit.

Play Within Yourself

The legendary Patty Berg, one of the founding members of the LPGA in 1950, was a teenager in 1935. She was invited to play in an exhibition game with Walter Hogan, a super-star golfer at that time. "I was very tense and couldn't hit anything straight," she later told a reporter. "I was in the rough all day and I hit 5 people in the crowd on the first 9 holes. My father was so busy passing out his business card for insurance purposes given all the people I'd hit, he was on his knees helping people to get back up, more than on his feet watching me. The First Aid tent was busier than the pop stand. My family and friends didn't want to admit they knew me."

Witty, feisty and yet so down-to-earth, she gave me the best advice when I participated in the Pat Bradley Thyroid Foundation Pro-Am quite a few years ago at Eastward Ho on Cape Cod in Massachusetts. Addressing a gallery of anxious amateurs who were about to tee up with an LPGA player in every foursome, Patty turned to us with some funny things to say and concluded her welcoming remarks by adding, with a wave of her hand, "Always remember to play within yourself."

At that moment, golf took on a whole new meaning for me. A calm came over me that allowed me to just be myself out there. If I have a good round, that is wonderful. If I stink up the joint, that is OK as well. I wasn't making my living as a professional golfer. I was just one of millions who have found profound joy in the game. If I shot 79 or 109, I wasn't going to be judged on my ability to strike the ball. Oddly enough, I am capable of posting both! I call it Cheryl's Psycho Golf.

I would try to never again feel embarrassed after hitting a bad shot. Everyone hits a bad shot now and then, even the Professionals. I no longer worried when someone used a pitching wedge as I stood near the same spot clutching my 9-iron. I had just received "The Sermon on the Mount" and all was right in my universe.

As we made our way to our starting tee that day, I watched as the men in my group teed it up at the back tee, then our LPGA Pro, Pat Bradley, hit from the whites. Then I strolled happily to the forward tee and hit a good drive down the middle. We used my drive on the first hole. Woo Hoo! As an aside here, you will almost always be lauded when you hit a long drive from the forward tees if you are the only player in your Scramble foursome hitting from those tees. So don't be overly impressed by my bravado. The forward tees were really, really forward.

The moral of the story is this: be yourself on the course. Set realistic goals and don't let a score define you. Don't put undue pressure on yourself to perform the way other players perform. Think in terms of playing to the best of your ability. Your skills will come with time, practice, and patience.

Be Realistic

Set realistic goals for yourself. At the end of the day, no one really cares about how the other people played. We are all lone wolves out there, playing against the course and working to attain our "personal pars".

Another observation Kathy shared with me is the difference between Trying Hard and Trying Too Hard. There is everything right about trying hard like taking lessons, playing regularly and making time to practice. It demonstrates you are serious about learning and investing your time in golf. Maintaining realistic expectations while enjoying the process of learning the game, and having fun is the best formula for you as a new player.

On the other hand, trying *too* hard is wanting to shoot 75 your first time on the golf course. It will be very disappointing when your score is 150. Becoming a golfer is like planting a garden. You begin by enriching the soil, then choosing the plants that will do well in either sun or shade. You will water those plants, pull out the weeds and give them fertilizer so they can grow and thrive. But a good garden, like a good golf game, takes time, effort and patience. Your blooms don't come overnight, but with diligent care, you will watch them grow and flourish.

Take your time with your game. Set your goals with your Instructor and enjoy the process. Your game will blossom and you will be able to enjoy the results of your efforts. I am using a gardening analogy here to gently remind you to take your time and smell the flowers along the way.

Kathy Hart Wood told me that gaining confidence in golf is not a linear process. It is more like a see-saw. Some days your confidence level is high while other days, it might be low. There are so many emotions we experience in golf: joy, elation, anger, fear, pressure, anxiety and worry. It is normal and it is all part of the game, just as these emotions affect us in our daily lives, they accompany us to the golf course. Every mistake we make should not be seen as a negative. It should be seen as part of the learning process. You are the only person who can allow yourself to see mistakes in this light.

"Play with the talent you have at this given time and tell yourself you are enough", Kathy told me as we ended our interview. Words of wisdom from a lady who knows her stuff.

Personal Par

As a new golfer, think about having a "personal par". Your personal par is what *you* consider a hole well-played. If you get a 7 on a long Par 4, then let a 7 be your personal par for a while. If we put too much pressure on ourselves to score well, then some of the joy of playing is stolen from us. As you improve, then maybe a 6 on that same long Par 4 becomes your new personal par. Whatever we can do to keep our expectations in line with our abilities will afford us the pleasure the game offers.

Dealing with Cheaters and Other Miscreants

When someone in your group is cheating, you can only point out the rule that addresses the particular situation or help to recount the number of strokes if her score is incorrect. If someone sees that you know and follow the rules, fair play will prevail. If you are with friends playing casually, let it go for the time, but have a quiet aside after the round. Your friend might not know that particular rule yet and you saved her from the embarrassment of being called out.

However, if you are playing in a tournament of any kind, and you agree not to call a rules infraction against yourself or your fellow competitor, you will both be disqualified for agreeing to break a rule. An issue we do not need to concern ourselves with just yet.

We can overlook bad shots and bad golf days, but it's harder to ignore poor sports, sore losers and let's toss in arrogant winners as well. There is simply no room in the business golf world for this kind of boorish behavior.

Just as good manners are important in our everyday lives, good manners are also extremely important on the golf course. While it is highly unlikely that you'll be faced with a real monster on the course, it could happen. Tell yourself it's just 4 hours and then cross that person's name off your golf buddy list. Life is too short and golf is too much fun to put up with nonsense, especially when you are trying to learn the game. If you have to talk to someone about unsportsmanlike conduct, do it after the round, in private, but think twice about addressing it during the round. All that will accomplish is adding fuel to an already out-of-control fire.

If someone is complaining or making excuses after every poor shot, chances are that person is not a very good golfer to begin with, which is not the crux of the problem. But if a player analyzes every shot with "I should have done this or I meant to do that," and then asks you if you can see what she is doing wrong, don't be tempted to weigh in. Giving a lesson on the course is not your job. It takes up too much time, and if your advice doesn't work immediately, then you have made yourself responsible for tinkering with that person's game. You are therefore responsible, in her mind, for all ensuing poor shots. Fixing playing problems is the job of the Golf Professional. As I remind myself several times a day on a plethora of issues from family to business, "Stay in Your Lane."

As women, we want to help, to make things better, to fix things, to make it right. On the golf course, we just need to play our own game, to play within ourselves. That is not to say we cannot be sympathetic and supportive of the player who is struggling. I am just suggesting we develop the ability to remain neutral during the round.

All athletes must learn not only physical discipline but mental discipline as well. If nothing else, golf demands self-control. While many people think golf builds character, I am of the opinion that golf also reveals character. Being able to remain positive and unruffled when your game seems to be falling to pieces is very important if you intend to get refocused and concentrate on making your next shot a solid one. Give yourself a mental mulligan and just keep trying.

The Amateur Who Thinks He's a Pro

I have often played in foursomes with new faces. There was sometimes a fellow who thought he was going to teach me a thing or two about how to play golf. "You should turn this way," or "You should come down on the ball harder." I've heard enough for a lifetime, and the best way to stop it immediately is to politely say you are working with a Golf Professional. Or what of the man who picks up your 5-foot putt, telling you it's good because there's a foursome behind you? He then proceeds to stand over his 2-footer for 4 minutes as though $50,000 depended on it ... and misses? Doesn't it make you wonder exactly *why* that foursome was right behind you? I have to admit, this was common 25 years ago. Much to their credit, the male golfers today are much more considerate and welcoming.

I think when we end up in a foursome with three men that we have only met on the first tee, their testosterone spikes and they reckon they are going to show off just a wee bit. They tee up from the back tees and take mighty swings. Rarely does the ball go straight. I will say nothing and just proceed to my forward tee. My drive goes straight down the middle. The men say in a barely audible voice, "Nice drive" as they head to the rough to search for their balls. By the fifth hole, they are asking what my handicap is, how long I have played, what I do for a living and if I have any friends or sisters who are single and play like me. By the 12th hole, we have bonded and they have accepted me as an equal. At the 19th hole they shared they had no idea "playing with a woman" could be so much fun.

While they might play in a charity outing five times a year, and take a golf trip with a buddy for a week twice a year, I am playing or practicing a least five times a week. And therein, my friends lies the difference.

The late Mike Royko, syndicated columnist, had me in fits of laughter with an article he wrote for *The Boston Herald* ages ago. He described a woman who told her husband she wanted to take golf lessons. "What for?" he asked. "I can teach you anything you want to know."

"I already know how to hit a ball into the water," she retorted.

We'll sum this up by saying there are a lot of moving parts when you strive to become a golfer. Developing all the skills you need to navigate your growth takes time and patience. You will find your circle of friends who will join you in your journey. When you get to the 19th hole, you certainly won't be at a loss for things to talk about. Especially if you recently played in a foursome with some new faces.

"Why the long face, Shirley?"

"My husband says I must choose between him and golf."

"Oh dear. I am so sorry to hear this."

"Me, too. I'm really going to miss him."

From *A Round of Golf Jokes* by Bill Stott

Chapter 6

Private Club Membership

Your Ultimate Goal

Research, Research, Research

Selecting a private golf or country club is a serious undertaking. You have some homework to do and connections to make for sponsorship before you write the first big check. Being a member of a private club is like finding the right community in which to live and raise your family, so you need to know as much as possible about this "community" before you buy. What is the initiation fee? What are the quarterly dues? What are the food minimums? What is the club's mission statement? What is the long-term strategic plan? Are there limitations about the club? By limitations, I mean does the club offer just golf? Many clubs today have a pool, tennis, pickle ball, gym and daycare. Does it have a good Junior Golf Program so your kids can become involved? Is it family-oriented or does it have a more corporate culture? Is it the most exclusive or most expensive club? Does it have a caddy program? What are the membership categories? How long is the Wait List for golf?

Just as you researched the town or city you live in to ensure it meets your needs, you will want to determine if this golf club and its amenities meet your needs before you join.

In order to join a private club, you will need to be sponsored. There will be a Membership Application to complete. Supporting letters must be submitted from several members who will sponsor you and are members in good standing. They will want to meet with you before they send their endorsement. Once that step is completed, you will have an interview with a member or members of the Membership Committee and then a vote will be taken by the Board of Directors.

If you are active in your local business community, it is not terribly difficult to be introduced to a private club through friends, relatives or business associates who are members there. Sometimes you'll have the good fortune to be invited to a meeting, a social function, or a charity or corporate golf outing which will give you a chance to play the course and to view the interior of the club. You will have an opportunity to see the locker room, lounge, and dining facilities. By the end of the day, you'll have a good idea as to the difficulty and condition of the golf course, how well the club is managed and the quality of the food and service coming from the kitchen. The kind of service you receive from the Bag Drop, Pro Shop and other staff members will also give you a feeling for how the club meets its mission statement. Today's private clubs are very much mission-driven, so it is safe to say you can expect an exceptional experience no matter where you join.

Learning how to play golf will seem easy compared to finding out about the inner workings of some private equity clubs before becoming a member. The word "private" refers as much to the attitude of the club's leaders and how their club is run as it does to the fact that the club house and course are not open to the public.

Equity vs Non-Equity

There are two types of private club models. With an Equity membership, you'll own a portion of the club, along with the other members. These are the most exclusive and most expensive clubs to join. The initiation fee can be as low as $25,000 or up to $250,000 or even $1,000,000, none of which is refundable should you leave. There will be dues and food minimums and other charges like golf cart usage, a locker fee, bag storage charge and the like. An Equity club elects a Board of Directors from the senior membership to oversee the long-range planning and operation of the club. A General Manager handles the day-to-day issues. The tax status of an Equity club is non-profit, therefore the Club strives to balance operating revenues and expenses, but not generate a profit.

In a Non-Equity Club, all of the amenities are owned by an entity other than the members and the facility is managed by industry-specific professionals with the intention of making a profit. So if you don't want a big buy-in number and the thought of serving on yet another volunteer board of directors isn't for you, this may well be the right choice. There are still quarterly dues and food minimums, but you have dodged a large initiation fee.

Different Levels of Membership, Different Costs

As you continue to gather information on the Equity club you are interested in joining, you will want to find out what exactly your investment will be. What is the initiation fee? What are the annual dues? What are the club's bylaws with regard to divorce? Can you stay if you and your husband/partner split up? Can you have a full membership in the event of your spouse's death? What are the monthly food minimums? Are the pool and tennis extra? Are they planning to remodel the club house or the golf course in the near future? If yes, you can expect an assessment. It seems to be "yes" on assessments everywhere recently, as golf has increased in popularity. Clubs, just like businesses, compete to win your business. So if a new pool or tennis center brings in more members, it will be built. You will be assessed.

All of these financial questions are essential in determining if this is the place for you. Also, in the event of a serious injury, onset of health problems, or if you are moving or being transferred and are no longer able to maintain your Equity membership, you must understand that no initiation money paid will be returned to you. Every private club is different because the rules and regulations are established by the members (Equity Club) or the corporation (Non-Equity Club). Be sure to get all the facts upfront.

How Long is the Wait List?

Once you have determined that this is the Club for you, it is important to get an idea of how long it will take before you become a golf member. Some newer clubs may have a waiting list of just a few months while other, more established clubs, have a five years, ten years or even longer waiting list.

The Probation Period

Most clubs have a probation period for all new members to make sure it's a good fit all the way around. A probation period could be as brief as ninety days or it could be as long as one year. As previously noted, Equity clubs require at least one sponsor and more likely three sponsors. The members who are sponsoring you should take an interest in getting you settled and introduced. They will help you to acclimate and serve as your go-to for questions. Failing the probation period is very, very rare. But make no mistake, it happens. You have to be a total nut case to flunk out, but as we all know, some people think they are entitled and above the law, or in this case, the by-laws.

Once the probation period is over (it sounds more intimidating than it is) you should be well-established and enjoying the club and its amenities. If there is a long waiting list for full golf privileges, perhaps you will be able to play once or twice a month with or without a member. Maybe you can play late afternoon on weekdays or in some of the 9-hole Scotches. It's a great way to meet your fellow members. These events usually start around 5 pm and have an easy format followed by dinner.

Just make sure you know what you can and cannot do and follow all the rules pertaining to the club house, golf course and grounds. Nothing will get you into hot water faster than breaking the rules. As I mentioned earlier, golf and country clubs are homogeneous societies. The nail that sticks out will be hammered down. I don't mean this in a negative way. Clubs have rules from dress code to conduct on the course. These rules and codes are meant to keep everything in this small "community" orderly, polite and civilized.

Taking a Stand

I was a History major in college. I believe history teaches us how our present came to be and it is a useful gauge to help us to anticipate and prepare for what might happen in the future. You know the old adage that those who do not learn from history are doomed to repeat it? In keeping with my promise to Susan Bond-Philo not to "shrink or pink" this book, I have decided to share some golf history featuring events that dramatically changed how golf clubs treat women today.

To a young executive reading this book, what follows may sound unfathomable in the DEI world of today. To women in my generation, we know these are events that actually happened. It saddens me to write about this. I have taken this section out and put it back in more times than I care to share, asking myself if this is relevant. Will it resonate with my readers? At the end of the day, I decided to take a chance with the belief you should know how it was for women and minorities at golf clubs "back then", you know, before you were born.

The following stories are taken from the late-Marcia Chambers' extraordinary and gutsy book, *Unplayable Lie: The Untold Story of Women and Discrimination in American Golf.* (Pocket Books, 1995)

It's meaningful to see change that comes willingly from the top. Once again, looking for examples of good corporate citizenship, here is a snapshot of actions taken by two top corporate leaders to end discrimination at their private golf clubs decades ago and without prompting or pressure. They were way ahead of their time.

When Paul H. O'Neill became Chairman of the Aluminum Company of America in 1987, he learned that one of the perks of running Alcoa was a membership at Laurel Valley Golf Club in Ligonier, Pennsylvania. According to *The Washington Post*, when he inquired if the club admitted women and blacks as members, and was told, "No," he refused to join. But he didn't stop there. The company adopted a policy that it would not pay dues for any of its executives to organizations that discriminated, or reimburse expenses incurred at such clubs.

Here is another excerpt from Marcia's book:

In 1994, John F. Smith, Jr., President and CEO of General Motors, resigned from Bloomfield Hills Country Club in Michigan, long an exclusive bastion of the auto industry's top executives, because Roy S. Roberts, a black vice president, was rejected for membership. This was not racism, the club's president said. But he offered no other reason for the action.

After Mr. Smith resigned from Bloomfield Hills, his story could be found in the major newspapers and TV shows.

Back in the 50s, 60s and 70s

Historically, country clubs have been for well-to-do men. Their wives did not have careers outside of the home. They raised a family, looked stylish and spent time at the club playing golf, tennis and bridge. There were some exceptions, but this was the general description of country club life back then.

Some rooms in the club house did not allow women. Some tee times (the best ones) were reserved for the men. Life in general was like "Father Knows Best" (there I go with black and white television again) and it worked because everyone was culturally on the same page. Think homogenous society here. The wives served on the garden committee or the decorating committee, but never on the Capital Planning Committee or the Green Committee. If you were a woman who won the Women's Club Championship, nothing much was made of it. No one was there to talk to talented junior girl golfers about college golf scholarships. The LPGA was in its infancy (1950) and the women who toured did not arrive in private jets like the PGA superstars of today. They arrived in groups of three or four women who traveled together in beat up station wagons, shared the least expensive hotel rooms and played for a fraction of the purse that the Professionals of today enjoy.

Title VII of the Civil Rights Act of 1964 started the proverbial golf ball rolling for women, by barring sex discrimination in the workplace. However, there is an exemption in the Act that allows bona fide private clubs to discriminate in their membership activities. I will not go into detail here as I am not a legal scholar by any stretch, but suffice to say that for years many private golf clubs had circled the wagons to keep women and other minorities on the outside. When our high courts considered the value of equality, they also considered the rights of privacy and freedom of association, ruling that private clubs, of any nature, were exempt from the Civil Rights Act of 1964.

Then, in 1972, Title IX of the Education Amendments put our institutions of higher learning on notice that the federal funds they received for athletic programs must be used equally between men and women.

Despite the entrance of women into "men only" schools, they were not made to feel welcome and the blatant discrimination against women in both academia and the business world helped to rekindle the Feminist Movement. Smoldering since the suffragists rocked the nation in the infancy of the last century, The Women's Liberation Movement demanded that women be treated equally. Please note here that it took until 1920 for the 19th Amendment to the US Constitution to be ratified, which gave women the right to vote. So when I say we have been at this a while, I am not joking.

Gloria Steinem founded *Ms* magazine in 1971. It covered the inequalities of women in education, the workplace and the voting booth. It has taken women decades and decades of hard work and "leaning in" to produce the gains we enjoy today in the business, political and academic worlds. But some country clubs were still culturally in the fifties. So it has remained that most of the men have preferred weekend morning tee times while the ladies have weekend afternoons. It is the men who hold office while it is the ladies who decorate the club house for parties. It is too often that the men decide where the forward tees shall be placed; it is the women who must hit from them.

Civilized Discourse

Having read to this point, if you are now of the opinion that golf clubs are male-dominated bastions, take heart. It's not like this everywhere. Stephanie Freeman, a resident of Weston, Connecticut, with a background in market research, has happily and successfully served not only on the board of her club, Redding Country Club in Redding, CT, she also served as President.

Stephanie was the second woman on the board and she served on various committees before becoming President. I spoke with her by phone some years ago as she began, "Ours is a family-oriented club. It's not stuffy and it is very female-friendly."

Redding had the "weekend morning tee time for working women" issue, just as hundreds of clubs do today.

"One club in our area decided to handle this issue by allowing one person in a family to play before noon on Saturday and Sunday. Then it was up to the couple to decide how to use that time," Stephanie said. "When the same issue came before our board at

Redding, unlimited tee times were voted in, albeit by a narrow margin. We now have a 'one family, one vote' rule, so that both the husband and wife or partners have a say in how the club is operated and how expenditures are to be made," she continued. "They just have to be of one mind before the vote is cast."

When I asked Stephanie if it made sense for female members (or any member) to sue their club for equal status, she felt that it should be a last resort and only after good faith negotiations have failed. She maintained that the way her club handled parity diffused any problems before things got out of control.

Keep in mind, when you are a member of a private equity club that is sued by a fellow member, the money to pay legal fees and the potential for a large judgment against the club will be borne by all members of the club. The money paid will most likely require an assessment. The vast majority of the members, whether they agree with you or not, will not be on your side.

Uncivilized Discourse

Sadly, not all golf clubs were able to settle these parity issues so easily and amicably. The year was 1988 and the club was in Old Brookville, Long Island, New York. Again, drawing from the late-Marcia Chambers' book, the following story is taken from *Unplayable Lie: The Untold Story of Women and Discrimination in American Golf.* I would add a note of caution here, this is an *extreme* example. I would rate it PG13 and will hasten to add that this will make you squirm in your seat. It is *only* because of these kinds of heroic actions that women's golf has not only survived but indeed has flourished in the ensuing years.

After pressing club officials for weeks, Lee Lowell had finally received permission from the Club's management to tee off early one weekend morning. She was a full member; the first woman at the club in that category. She wondered how hard that could be for the men, who were so used to their special weekend tee times. But that system could not last forever. This was America. It was 1988. It would be okay. She was a good golfer.

She and her husband had joined Cedar Brook a few months before. She played there mainly in the summer and autumn months. For the remainder of the year, the couple lived in Florida and were members of a club that had no restrictions on tee times. She hated the tee restrictions at Cedar Brook and had vowed to change them when she joined. One could see why. On weekends the pecking order put women out last. First men members teed off. Then men members with male guests. Then honeymooners, of all things. And finally, 'Lady members with or without guests.'

This day, Mrs. Lowell, a former art teacher, faced a special obstacle. She would be playing in a shotgun. A shotgun means golfers begin play simultaneously from all eighteen holes in order to get play moving quickly and to end the round together. What traditionally follows is a lunch for all of the players. Had it not rained the previous day, and had she gone out with women she knew, events might have turned out differently. As it was, she was paired with two male members she did not know.

She arrived at the seventeenth tee. "The two gentlemen I was supposed to play with told me they wouldn't play with me." She was bewildered, stunned; she didn't know what to do or say. She played the hole alone and went on to the eighteenth tee.

It was there that she met up with the chairman of the men's golf committee. He and a couple of other men were standing in the middle of the fairway, obviously unaware that she had been given permission to play. From where she stood it seemed they were trying to stop play. Mrs. Lowell couldn't understand what was going on. Suddenly, one of the men erupted like Mt. Vesuvius. He began yelling obscenities at her and was joined by others. "They kept screaming I could not play," Mrs. Lowell said. Rather than keep to the order of the game and go to the first tee as required, Lee Lowell headed for what she thought was safer ground, the sixteenth tee. It was empty.

The men revved up their golf carts and went after her. They cursed at Lowell from 150 yards away. Undaunted, she teed off. As she drove her cart to her ball, a man walked up to it, picked it up, and put it in his pocket. He continued to curse at her. She fled again, now to the second tee. As she teed it up, a posse of golfers appeared on the horizon, racing toward her in the golf carts. They stopped and got out in front of her. One of them unzipped his fly and peed in front of her. The Golf Chairman, who would have needed the Green Berets to stop him now, waved the ball he had picked up on the sixteenth hole and threw it at her. He shook his finger in my face and said to me, 'You will never hit another golf here ball again.' Still screaming at her, he kicked her ball off the tee.

Now she was really terrified. She tried not to show it, saying to herself, "Okay, I'll just leave." She took off in her golf cart. But this was not to be. As if in Dodge City, the golf posse, led by the fearless Golf Chairman, pursued her up and down the fairways in a frenzied golf cart chase.

Finally, they encircled her. The course appeared to fall silent. "I was alone. But I was determined not to let them run me off," she said. "Yet I was scared. I felt like a child who was afraid of being maimed or hurt. I felt the rage in these men. They reduced me to a child. That's what angers me. I've raised my children, I got myself educated, yet that man diminished me. And where was I? In a wealthy country on the fairways of a private golf club.

How should they resolve what would later be described in court as Lowell's **"gender invasion"**?

While the men were busy discussing their next move, she took off, playing the empty tees, moving quickly from seven to eight, then nine and onto one and five. Afterward, she went to the Ladies' Locker Room and cried. "I love golf and that's what broke my heart.", she said.

A few hours later, the club manager telephoned her at home. She learned that, without ever hearing her side, the golf committee, some of whom had chased her in their carts, had now suspended her for two weeks. Lowell's life at the club would never be the same. They stayed on, but it wasn't pleasant. Her friends ignored her.

She tried to stay active in the club. She signed up, not surprisingly, for the grievance committee. Learning that, the club's officials disbanded the grievance committee. Her scientist husband was denigrated, too. He would be summoned from lunch to the locker room and no one was there. Both received threatening telephone calls at home. "You better not play or your life is at stake," said one caller.

Not until after a long court battle, and several hearings covering some seven years, did Mrs. Lowell find peace. They eventually joined another New York club that had no restrictions on women. As a result of the incident, Cedar Brook has made some dramatic reformations, including the establishment of a mixed grille room and allowing equal tee time access on weekend mornings.

What can one say about a story like what happened in NY? It is laughable. It is sad. It is hard to believe, and yet, there it is in black and white on the page. We go from civilized discourse resulting in parity in Connecticut from sound leadership to New York and a Quentin Tarantinoesque horror show. If you think just playing golf is an emotional see-saw, I have now shared of bit of the history of how women have had to fight for every crumb of equality in the golf club world.

How sad that events had to take such a shameful (and expensive) turn to get a private club to update its unfair practices toward a Full Member female. It is even sadder when one considers that so often members of private clubs are the business leaders of their community. If their actions on the golf course reflected their true feelings about women, what chance did women really have as they looked for career opportunities in the companies that they ran?

And Now, the Good News

While there are still a handful of private golf clubs that do not admit women, we shall set that discussion aside, and look at the bigger and better picture. Golf and golf club memberships have become more attractive and attainable for many people who come from a variety of professions, from white-collar to blue-collar and a plethora of ethnic backgrounds. More and more, private clubs are run by people who have a pulse on America's love of golf and know how to package and present the Country Club or Golf Club lifestyle and experience. They have skillfully targeted two-income professional couples, many with small children. They welcome beginners and even those in "middle age" and beyond, who want to learn how to play. They have made golf club membership easy, non-threatening, equal and completely transparent.

Entertaining friends, family and clients at your club will lead you to new business opportunities as you come to know more and more of the members. Meeting for dinner at your club after a hectic day can be a great way to unwind. You can get a tee time with little or no difficulty, especially on the weekends and the condition of the course and club house will always be top notch. You will play in organized golf events just by clicking on the reservation tab on the club's website. In the long run, membership in a private club should be a very personally satisfying and financially rewarding investment.

For example, ClubCorp which now positions itself in the marketplace as "Invited" offers over 204 Clubs across the country and boasts 430,000 members. I love how they summed up their activities for 2022:

28,000 new members

1,800 Weddings celebrated

4.75 million rounds of golf played

7.1 million meals enjoyed

60,000 member events hosted

144 blood drives hosted

Now that is a company that "gets it". They see the future of golf as diversified, equal and inclusive and they take an active role in the communities they serve. They are *good corporate citizens* because they support the communities they serve, all the while ensuring the growth of the great game of golf, keeping it accessible to all.

The Game for a Lifetime

Golf is supposed to be fun, first and foremost. The sooner we learn not to take ourselves too seriously on the course, the sooner we will relax and enjoy not only the great game, but the fine company and the beautiful surroundings with which we have been blessed. Golf is not, as Mark Twain said, "A good walk spoiled." No, to me, it is a wonderful way to enjoy a clear blue sky on a lovely summer day, to smell the fragrance of newly opening buds floating over a gentle spring breeze or the chill in the autumn air that makes your cheeks flush and your toes a little tingly. I feel so alive when I am on the golf course. I love watching a red-wing hawk float gracefully overhead and I readily admit to cooing over new ducklings, all small and fuzzy, as they make their way to the water as a bossy, squawking mother duck leads the brood. I even love to see – from a healthy distance – an alligator slipping into the pond as it senses the approach of humans and their noisy golf carts. Don't misunderstand me. I am not just loving nature, I am still focusing on making purposeful shots and scoring well, but I have learned how to find the balance of a good game and a happy day.

I enjoy playing with my friends, as we rib each other and take the temperature of our lives, making sure we are all doing well. I also like playing with new people at my clubs, because they'll be strangers for only a hole or two. I'll find some silly thing to say and everyone will laugh and with that burst of laughter, we'll be on our way to becoming friends.

I really appreciate every game because I am now of a certain age and on the Back Nine of my life. I am happy to be looking down at the tee instead of looking up at it if you know what I mean. Enjoy each time you get to play golf. Goodness knows, we've all spent enough time at our desks on sunny days and burned the midnight oil to finish a report or prepare for a meeting. Don't forget the times spent at the airport, stuck on the tarmac on a hot day, or having your flight canceled. I will never forget the traffic jams that took hours to get through. During one New England blizzard, my one-hour commute took over three hours. Remember the business trip hotel rooms that looked good when we booked online and turned out to be 'Elvis on Velvet' ugly. The biggest challenge we all have shared was dealing with Covid-19 and all the misery that the virus brought.

We've worked hard and sacrificed to get to where we are in life. So when it's time to go out and play golf, don't forget to place a bit more emphasis on the "play" part! The golf part will come in good time.

Chapter 7

Mentoring

Helping Other Women to Use Golf as a Business Tool

In the many decades that I have been involved in the business world, I have had the good fortune to meet some wonderful people who took an interest in my career. I also joined and actively participated in local membership or trade associations that were either directly tied to the business I was in, or which brought me into contact with people I wanted to meet to further my own career ambitions.

In that process, I met dozens of men and women who were willing to share their knowledge and expertise, or who were able to introduce me to the people with whom I wanted to do business. The fastest way to achieve your goals is to have a mentor who is willing to help you avoid the mistakes they themselves may have made or have seen others make. A good mentor will always have your back covered and your success in mind.

Across the country, numerous business associations create and provide "Women's Business Networks" thus fostering networking and mentoring among their members. On the whole, they are successful because they give younger female executives access to seasoned, successful female executives and community leaders. Yet, I have heard some women sniff at the prospect of joining women-only business groups. They argue that they have worked very hard to attain their own senior positions and that these single-sex associations are too narrow. They claim they do not want to be singled out as "women executives," they just want to be known as executives.

While I understand the challenges associated with acquiring and maintaining senior-level positions, I wonder if we sometimes either consciously or subconsciously close the door behind us as soon as we reach the C-Suite. Is it the corporate culture? Or is it that the highest level business leaders have a team around them who screen calls, scrutinize mail and "gatekeep" with military precision in their efforts to insulate "the boss" from the mundane in order to economize our time?

I would urge women, whether they are corporate executives or entrepreneurs, to take an interest in women who are starting to "climb the ladder" by being a mentor and helping them to negotiate the "first rung". To my way of thinking, that means getting those women involved in golf, if they are amenable. As an established executive who plays golf, anything you can do to help other women accelerate their learning process and prepare them to take up golf is as important as giving them the benefit of your experience in the business world. Introducing our female business associates to other women who play helps them plug right into the "old girl's network" and helps them to break the grass ceiling. It prepares them to play with men and to enter the inner sanctum of elite decision-makers and business leaders.

In fact, if you are of the mind that more women in your company should play golf, but are unsure of how to get started, you might consider encouraging your company to underwrite a day-long clinic and include some of your high-ranking female executives and perhaps a few female clients. I know of many companies and financial institutions that have done just that with great success.

Katherine Cohane, VP with American Express participated in her company's semi-annual clinic and was interviewed by Vicki Salemi, a reporter with *The New York Post*. Here are some excerpts from the excellent article written by Ms. Salemi.

"Conversations at the clinic don't immediately focus on work," says Cohane. "We begin discussing each other's experiences playing golf. We might then ease into a more natural conversation about family and friends."

Linda Zukauckas, an EVP and Deputy CFO at American Express at that time, launched these clinics in 2010 saying, "This deeper connection has helped me better understand what Cohane and her colleagues need from me as a leader. As a result (of the clinics) our working relationship is stronger and more impactful. The golf course is where professionals build camaraderie and often hear about 'under the radar' opportunities. We are leveling the playing field and helping those women striving to reach the C-suite or Boardroom."

Salemi reported that the clinics consisted of 75 women from VP level and above and included golf instruction and a networking luncheon with an executive speaker.

The story continued with Susan M. Moss, Esq., a partner at a Midtown Manhattan law firm. "Playing golf in legal networking is hugely important," Ms. Moss said. By playing with members of the Women's Bar Association, she got to know some of the members very well and those golf outings "helped me settle cases when difficult issues arose."

Delphine Lincy, another executive featured in the interview commented, "Getting better at golf definitely helps your confidence. From the early years, when I stepped up to the first tee, knowing I would hit the ball all over the place, men would not want to play with me", Lincy told Ms. Salemi. "I pushed through humiliation, intimidation and embarrassment to become better than them," Lincy added that the sport, in addition to skill, also emphasizes honesty and integrity as the fundamentals of the game.

I was watching CNBC and there was a segment on how a nationally-known financial services company was paying for one (yes, just one) of its female executives to take golf lessons. A huge company with thousands of capable women on the payroll was paving the way (and paying the way) for just one woman. Not exactly what I would call a good start. Can you imagine the pressure she must have felt to improve quickly? Hey fellas, get that lady some golf friends. Call Linda Zukauckas, she'll give you the scoop on how it's done.

If you are in the driver's seat in your company and you want to do something to boost morale among your golfing women executives, consider arranging golf clinics or a series of private lessons. Send the beginners to a Golf Camp. Do whatever you can to get them up and running. Send your best players to corporate or charity golf outings, but not as a foursome. Why, you ask? Split them up so they can play with three guests each and hopefully establish new avenues for business.

If you really want to establish yourself as a golf mentor who cares, invite beginners out occasionally for 9 holes at an easy course. While you won't be able to give lessons on the mechanics of the game, you can certainly show them the ropes by helping them to learn the rules and etiquette.

I did just that for one of my friends. Susan Michaels, an insurance executive and her attorney husband, Stephan, kept their two practices humming along for many decades under one roof. While Stephan played a little golf, Susan spent more time in the office. They joined Woodland Golf Club in Auburndale, Massachusetts at the same time I did, over 30 years ago. While we were great friends, Susan was a little nervous about golf, while I was more established in my game. She was happy to be a founding member of my Boston-area golf association for professional women and she loved attending the monthly networking dinners but had yet to pick up a club.

At the time, they were living in a high rise in downtown Boston and I took her aside one day and suggested that her summers would be rather lonely on the weekends because her husband would be off playing golf and she would be in the hot and steamy city. Susan knew if she wanted to participate in our club's many golf events and accompany her husband to his annual legal and insurance industry golf outings, she needed to add golf to her resume. She enrolled in the Novice Clinic that Susan Bond-Philo held for my golf association members at Wellesley Country Club and the rest, as they say, was history.

"I loved it!", she gushed over the phone the morning after her first lesson. She went on to become an avid golfer and now lives in Naples, Florida, in yet another high rise, and plays regularly at her club there. Doing something like that for a friend – igniting that lifelong love of golf - is the greatest joy in my life. We remain the closest of friends, even today, some 40 years later.

Clearly, as we become adults it is just plain hard to try something new, but every time we push ourselves out of our comfort zone, new brain cells fire up and we find that what we thought to be impossible is, in fact, quite achievable. I think it takes significant intestinal fortitude for a woman who is a high-ranking executive or leader in her field, to head for the lesson tee and become a "Rookie" as she takes on the job of learning how to use golf as a business tool.

Undeterred, Susan took lessons all summer long. Every day, she would either swing in front of a mirror at home, or she would head for the driving range at our club, which was just a short distance from her office, to hit balls and work on her game. She also told me she kept a club near her desk at work and would practice gripping the club over and over until it started to feel right. Lots of lessons later, a small fortune spent on golf clothes and equipment, and the most determined attitude I have ever seen, she started the next season with the club's WGA 9-hole group and quickly moved up to the 18-hole group. Since that time, she has played with her husband, with clients and friends, and has enjoyed many vacations and business trips that included golf. She created a circle of friends through golf that has lasted for many, many years.

Let's extend mentoring to our daughters, granddaughters and nieces, as well. If your daughter has an interest in golf, then help her get started by finding a Golf Professional for regular lessons, enroll her in golf camp and make time to play as a family. It can be a great way to watch your kids grow up and something that you will always be able to share together. If your daughter is a gifted junior golfer, I would urge you to look into the golf scholarships that are available from so many noteworthy colleges and universities. Oftentimes, those scholarship dollars go unused because parents are not aware of their availability. The point here is that if your daughter chooses to follow a professional path, whether it's business, law or science, golf will help her to succeed by opening some doors she might not otherwise pass through.

"I loathe golf advice. I loathe golf professionals. Everyone suggests; straighten this, twist that, look down, relax, swing, move your thumb up, move your thumb down. And all of this because the course designers and the pros are in collusion. One is paid to drive you mad by making the course impossible. The other is paid to drive you mad teaching you how to overcome the obstacles that shouldn't have been there in the first place. Relax. Roll with the system. Book in for another 10 lessons. You're nearly there…..."

Helen Richards from *Golf. A Good Walk Spoiled.*

Chapter 8

Rules and Etiquette

The First Woman Golfer?

Before we dive into this section, let me take a moment to tell you about the first female golfer. Mary, born in Scotland in 1542, was sent to France as a child. She was betrothed from childhood to Frances, a young boy who would someday be the King of France. You could call the arrangement a political joint venture to keep the two countries allied. Mary was fascinated by the game of golf while growing up there. (Golf might have been pronounced "gawff" back then.) Hanging around the castle all day just wasn't for her, so she passed her time chasing the little white ball around the French countryside. A young Cadet (pronounced kah-day) would be selected from the French military each time Mary played. That is where the term caddy originated. The young soldier was to carry her golf bag and ensure the safety of France's future Queen.

As time went on, Mary did indeed marry Frances and became Queen of France. Sadly, King Frances died not long after they were wed. Soon after, Mary's mother, the Queen of Scotland, died. Mary Queen of France returned to Scotland to assume the throne. We now know her from history as Mary, Queen of Scots.

Once settled on the Scottish throne, Mary resumed her love of chasing after the golf ball and married a distant cousin, Henry Stuart, Lord Darnley. It seems Lord Darnley did a bit of chasing himself. Only his pastime was chasing young maidens, not golf balls.

Mary Queen of Scots was having none of that. She soon took her own lover, David Riccio, who was murdered in her presence. Well, the Queen was not pleased with this development. Not long after poor Riccio's demise, the house where Lord Darnley dallied was blown up by a large gunpowder explosion and he was later found strangled in the garden.

How did Mary mourn her second husband's passing you might wonder? Why with a round of golf. It's good to be the Queen.

All this was happening during a time when the Elders of the Isles agreed that golf took the men away from archery practice, which was critical to national defense. It is rumored that Mary commissioned the construction of St. Andrews Links during her reign and continued her love of golf. Sadly, she was dethroned and kept prisoner for many years, accused of plotting the assassination of her cousin, the Queen of England.

Ultimately, Mary was beheaded in 1587 and women's golf went into a bit of a slump for the next 200 years.

Fast forward to 1744 when the first organized golf society was established in Scotland, which led to the birth of the Royal and Ancient Golf Club of Scotland. When the Rules of Golf torture and torment you, lay your blame "across the pond". But don't lose your head over it.

(I have taken a bit of literary license here solely for your amusement.)

How to Act Like a Pro Even if You're a Novice

The rules of golf are painstakingly written, updated and rewritten every four years. On the other hand, the equally important golf etiquette does not have an official handbook, and yet volumes have been dedicated to describing good manners on the course.

Every game we play has rules that must be followed. Golf is no exception. In fact, the rules of golf are sometimes difficult to interpret and understand. With rules and sub-rules, we shouldn't wonder why many of the Professional golfers call for help when they are unsure of a situation during a tournament. If a player is leading by one or two strokes, she certainly doesn't want to incur a penalty by breaking a rule she isn't sure about and risk losing the tournament. Don't be intimidated by the rules, be informed. Don't assume that everyone who plays knows or even follows the rules. You will earn the respect of your golf partners if you know at least a handful of the rules and practice the etiquette.

All this said, the most important thing for a new golfer to do when starting out is to play by her own rules. Have fun and just work on finding your favorite club and advancing the ball. Give yourself time to fall in love with the game first. Give yourself mulligans and permission to relax. Enjoy the fresh air and drink in the beauty of being outside. More than likely, you will play your first several rounds overwhelmed with hitting the ball, getting on the green and putting out. Hopefully, you will be guided by caring friends and family members who want you to love the game as much as they do. Please be kind to yourself and be patient. It takes some time to become a golfer. As I mentioned earlier, it's a marathon, not a sprint.

It's hard to imagine that in 1744, the first organized golf society in Scotland followed just thirteen rules. Those rules endured for another decade when they were adopted by the Royal and Ancient Golf Club of St. Andrews in Scotland in 1754. Today, there are nearly 3 times as many rules. In 1952, the USGA and the R&A (Royal and Ancient) came together and standardized the rules, with a new set published every four years, usually with some minor changes. The big change came in 1990 when the aforementioned groups settled upon a standard set of rules for the game. The biggest changes for today's golfers happened in 2019. These new rules made golf more user-friendly and offered many ways to speed up the pace of play. Being environmentally conscious, The

Official Rules of Golf is no longer printed. It is now available as an app on your cell phone or PC.

This chapter will present the key rules with some etiquette mixed in so that you can gain confidence quickly. Knowing the rules is not meant to turn you into a nasty nit-picker, but to enhance your enjoyment of the game and empower you to play with knowledge and confidence. This knowledge will be invaluable when you are ready to play with business associates or clients. Whether you are playing in leagues, amateur tournaments, or just with friends and colleagues, little things like knowing where to stand on the tee box and what to do when your ball goes in the water, will make life on the golf course much more enjoyable and relaxing. While we think of golf as a leisure time activity, it is first and foremost an ancient game of honor. Playing by the rules will boost your confidence and increase your respect for the game and its rich traditions. Just as important, practicing the etiquette of golf will earn you the respect of your fellow golfers.

There are times in golf, especially those relaxed rounds when we play with good friends when we don't follow every rule. A good example is playing golf in the Fall here in New England. There are red, yellow, orange and gold-hued leaves littered everywhere on the ground as our deciduous trees shed their foliage to make ready for winter. The groundskeepers usually blow those leaves into generous piles along the fairway sides before removing them. In my casual foursome, we announce the "leaf relief" rule on the first tee. After we have shuffled through a mound of leaves for a few moments, we just put a ball in play where we all agree it disappeared and keep playing. No penalty as we move along in our quest to get inside before it gets dark, too cold, or starts to drizzle. This rule is our own creation and not found in the Official Rules of Golf, but you are most welcome to use it when you play with your friends.

Let's be sensible about rules when we are out to have fun. If it is a busy day on the course with players directly in front of you and a foursome behind you, you may all agree to forego a "stroke and distance" penalty for a shot thought to be in play, when in fact it is lost or out-of-bounds once your group arrives to that area. Having a player trudge back to the area from where the ball was originally struck will just drive the group behind you crazy. Opt for the penalty (2 strokes) but skip the trip backwards (distance) and keep playing. Drop your ball on the edge of the fairway on the line where you believe the ball disappeared. Obviously, you cannot do this in a tournament or a match because all rules are in play and must be followed. To agree to break any rules in this situation will result in disqualification of all players involved in the agreement. In this case, the penalty will be 1 stroke because you will have to walk back to the original spot of the errant shot. Once again, give it time and it will all come together as you continue your life with golf. Just play by your own rules for now and have fun with the experience of being out on the course.

My philosophy has always been to try to encourage newer golfers by helping them to relax and laugh after a bad shot. Golf is hard enough when you're starting out that you don't need someone pointing out your every mistake. And believe me, there are plenty of mistakes to be made when you are a new golfer. I encourage people to take Mulligans and I give those 2-foot putts, especially if a new player has already made three putts. There will be plenty of time as they develop their skills to absorb many of the rules and learn more of the etiquette. These are the niceties that keep a round casual and relaxing, especially for newer golfers. I might take the player aside and ask if I could offer a suggestion on etiquette or if she would like me to explain the rule. Almost always, help is appreciated.

I do strongly feel that it is incumbent upon the more experienced players to mentor and support newer players. They need to think back to when they started playing and all the faux pas they committed. Funny thing about golfers, they won't remember how you played, but they will *always* remember how you treated them. Please do not extinguish the passion a new player has for golf with your impatience or indifference. Please be nice.

As your game develops and you become more proficient, should you be paired with someone who has a terrible swing, you may watch where the ball goes, but try not to watch the swing. There are some swings out there that look like a frog in a blender. Resist the urge to coach or correct. Just "stay in your lane" and play your own game.

I found this list of "rules for new golfers" from the PGA. How wonderful to see this august organization so dedicated and determined to make learning golf easier and less rigid. Here are some snippets from their "It's Okay Rules" campaign. It is brilliant and I wish we had this when I started playing those many years ago.

It's Okay Rules

- It's okay not to keep score.
- It's okay to play from the shortest tees or start at the 150-yard marker.
- It's okay to give yourself a better lie by rolling the ball around a little.
- It's okay to tee the ball up anywhere when you are first learning.
- It's okay to count swings only when you make contact with the ball.
- It's okay to throw the ball out of a bunker after one try.
- It's okay to forget about the ball that may be lost or out of bounds. It's okay to drop a ball where you think it might be… or where you wanted it to be.

- It's okay to play a scramble with your group - scrambles are very popular.
- It's okay to just chip and putt on a hole when you feel like it.
- It's okay to pick up in the middle of the hole and enjoy the outdoors and scenery.
- It's okay to skip a hole if you need a break.
- It's okay to play less than 9 or 18 holes and call it a round of golf.
- It's okay to move your ball away from the trees, rocks or very hilly lies.
- It's okay to hit the same club for the entire round while using a putter on the green.
- It's okay to play golf in your sneakers. Be comfortable.
- It's okay to get enthusiastic! (High-fives, fist pumps and big smiles are encouraged.)
- It's okay to talk on the golf course - enjoy a nice conversation or tell a few jokes.
- It's okay to play golf just for fun! Play the tees that make you the happiest.
- It's okay to laugh and have fun. There are no penalties for excessive laughing or high-fives on the golf course.
- It's okay to gamble some - and laugh even more.
- It's okay to remember friends more than your scores.
- It's okay that your love of the game lasts longer than that for a past "significant other".
- It's okay to quietly play your favorite music on every hole.
- It's okay to have your spouse or significant other outdrive you on every hole when they play from the forward tees.
- It's okay to turn off your cell phone while on the course.
- It's okay to "Drive for Show" - but not putt for dough.
- It's okay to create your own charity golf events to raise dollars for good causes.
- It's okay to be called a "golfer."

For more information geared to new golfers, visit the PGA website.

Once you have gained a comfort level and are ready to take a few more steps with golf, this chapter will help you to reach the next level. Not every rule will be covered here, but rather you will be given enough information to let you decide how to properly handle different situations that will inevitably arise as you make your way around the course. Because the rules and etiquette of golf are so closely intertwined, you'll find tips on how to conduct yourself on the course and around the club house in this section as well.

"I learned the game of golf playing in a league with men who delighted in teaching me the rules, one by one, after I broke them, one by one," said Bonnie A. Rafuse, President of Quality Journeys in Daytona Beach, Florida. It seems their delight, as she told me the story some years ago, came from adding one or two-stroke penalties to her scorecard. "Sometimes I had fun, sometimes I got frustrated. But I got better and I learned the rules because I wanted to compete against them."

While the rules of golf may seem complex and sometimes confusing at first glance, every player should try to know at least the key rules. When you have a command of the rules and etiquette, you will know how to handle the many incidents that can and will occur during just about every round.

Give yourself a pat on the back for sticking with this chapter and being so determined. Let's begin, as they say, at the beginning - on the first tee - and walk through the key rules all the way to the green. I think most avid golfers would agree that a newer player will be welcomed and encouraged if she knows a handful of the rules, practices the etiquette and, most importantly, moves along. If you lie 8 and the green is still 100 yards away, be a good sport and pick up your ball. We have all done it and there is absolutely no shame in it. It is just part of what happens when you are starting out as a new golfer. Hang in there, someone else in your group may have the same experience on the next hole. It's called a "Blow Up" hole. No one, not even the Professionals, is exempt. Jordan Speith, a PGA Champion, scored a 7 (quadruple bogey) on the Par 3 12th hole at Augusta during the 2016 Masters. On international television. Ouch.

Number of clubs

The first rule is an easy one. The number of clubs you may legally carry in your golf bag is 14. You certainly may carry fewer, as many new golfers do. A player with more than 14 clubs in her bag will receive a two-stroke penalty for every hole played with more than 14 clubs or could simply be disqualified from the competition.

I remember when I started playing, I owned a red vinyl Wilson golf bag and rattling around in it was a 3-wood, 7-8- and 9-irons, a pitching wedge, a sand wedge and a putter. I wish I still had that set, just for sentimental reasons. Just 7 clubs. At first, they all went about the same distance when I was lucky enough to get the ball airborne.

On the Tee

The Tee Box is an area that has been closely mowed and leveled. It has several sets of colored balls or markers. They can be painted or may be made of stone, wood, or whatever material the course designer has chosen. The tees you see way at the back of the teeing area are commonly referred to as "the tips" or the black tees. Those back tees are generally the domain of very low-handicap male players. The forward tees are what concern us in this book. Let's not call them the Ladies Tees or the Women's Tees. Ever. Never. No. No. No. They are simply the forward tees.

While you are waiting for your nod from the Starter to come to the first tee with your group, there are some "housekeeping" details that need to be addressed. Make sure introductions are made if you are playing with people who might not know each other. If you are with friends, and if you want to play some sort of game, decide on the bet and get the cards stroked. You certainly don't have to play a Nassau, or any other games that appear in Chapter 10. You can just play golf. All of these details can be decided on the driving range or practice green so that you are ready to go when you are called to the first tee.

The honor (who will tee off first) can be determined by tossing a tee in the air, with the players standing in a circle. The person to whom the tip of the tee points upon landing on the ground will hit first. Toss the tee two more times to finish the order. Or you can go off according to handicap, with the highest or lowest handicap hitting first. You can also put four balls in a hat and have one of the players pull them out one at a time to decide the order. Or you can also just agree to tee off in no particular order. There is no one way to decide the order unless you are playing in an organized tournament. In that case, the lowest handicap in the foursome will tee off first. Casual foursomes should always agree to play "ready golf" to keep the pace of play moving smoothly and efficiently throughout the round. We will go into more detail on "ready golf" in just a bit. If you are in an organized tournament, the player who finishes the previous hole with the fewest number of strokes will have "the honor" of going first on the next hole, and so on throughout the round. If the previous hole has been tied or halved (in match play), the person with the honor on the last hole would still retain the honor on the next hole. Once off the tee, the person who is "away" or in other words furthest from the flag stick, is the first to hit.

Carry two golf balls in your pocket at least for the first hole. I like to carry tees and balls in my right pocket and my ball marker and repair tool in my left pocket. That way, I never have to fumble around looking for what I need. There are few things that announce your status as a novice more pointedly than fumbling with tissues, lipstick, tees and what not, as you struggle to find a ball marker in your pockets. Remember, the players in your foursome are waiting to putt while you are trying to mark your ball. Keep in mind you are playing "ready golf" at *every* moment of the round. Every second wasted adds up to minutes over 9 or 18 holes and slows the pace of play. Some players use a magnet with a clip that attaches to the golf visor and they wear their ball markers that way. It won't take long to amass a colorful and fun collection of metal ball markers if you choose this way to carry your ball marker. These ball markers make great tee gifts along with whatever other items you add to the Welcome Bag if you are planning a guest day at your club. Many golf gloves have a small ball marker that snaps on the top of the glove. So you have some great options to be totally organized on the green.

Another suggestion with regard to golf balls is to use the same brand throughout the round. Announce the brand of your golf ball on the first tee. You have put your special mark on it to further help to identify your ball throughout the round. Knowing that you are using a Titleist 3 along with your special mark made by using a felt tip pen (you can use your initials, a circle, a triangle or any symbol to distinguish your ball from others on the course) reduces the risk of hitting the wrong ball during play and incurring a penalty. For example, if you hit the wrong ball in stroke play, it is a two-stroke penalty. If you hit the wrong ball in match play, you are out of the hole and the point for that hole goes to your opponent.

Let's discuss the tee box for a moment. When teeing your ball, you may stand anywhere between the markers and up to two club lengths behind them, but never in front of them. You may take your stance outside of the tee box, but your ball must be inside the tee box. You will incur a one-stroke penalty in stroke play if you tee up anywhere outside of the box. In match play, you will be asked to re-tee your ball or replay the shot without penalty. It only has to happen to you once and I feel certain you will never do it again. Don't hesitate to tee up a foot behind the markers. That way, you will never be questioned about being ahead of the markers.

Here's a helpful suggestion. I have seen quite a few novices try to put the tee into the ground first and then put the ball on top. It can be a struggle. Instead, try nesting the ball in your palm, with the cup of the tee under the ball and the shaft of the tee peg nested between your index and middle finger. Use the ball and tee as a "tool" to insert the tee into the ground.

Let's clear up a common misconception about knocking the ball off the tee while you are standing in the tee box. It does not count as a stroke and it does not incur a penalty. The ball is considered in play only when you have taken your stance, grounded your club and taken a stroke with the intention of hitting the ball.

You may also stop your swing at any point *before* hitting the ball, step back to collect your thoughts, and start over without penalty. We have seen Tiger Woods do that. However, if you intended to hit the ball, swung and missed it, that is called a "whiff" and is indeed a stroke that you must count. In fact, a whiff that occurs anywhere on the course from the tee and even on the green must be counted as a stroke. I guess we can all agree that is a good incentive to keep our eyes on the ball.

Every golfer should have a pre-shot routine. A pre-shot routine is a series of actions briefly performed each time before teeing off or hitting from anywhere on the course. Some players stand behind the ball and look down the fairway to select a point along an imaginary line to select their target. Some players take a most acceptable practice swing. On the etiquette side, taking more than one practice swing on every shot is not considered acceptable. However, if you are preparing for a shot to the green from thick rough, you might want to take a few practice swings to get a feel for how much "oomph" you need to get through the grass.

Whatever set-up routine you decide on, please do not develop the habit of standing over your ball too long. It doesn't do your game very much good. Overthinking usually results in a poor shot. It can be quite annoying to not only those in your foursome but the foursome playing behind you. Be decisive with your shots and club selections.

If you are playing with a caddy, he or she may not stand behind you to assist with alignment once you take your stance. The same holds true for your golf partner. You may discuss alignment and select a target together, but once you are ready to hit, you must do so without assistance.

Alignment

Just about all of us amateurs, seasoned or not, struggle with alignment. How many times do you think you are lined up straight as an arrow on the tee box and find your drive goes right?

Your Instructor will work on alignment during your lessons. You should also use the alignment sticks at the driving range if they are available. Otherwise, use two clubs from your golf bag. Choose your target on the driving range. Put one club on the ground across the toes of your shoes. Place the other club parallel on the other side of your ball. These are your "railroad tracks". Now, take a step back and see if you are headed to your target. Yes, I thought so. Just like me, you are aimed to the right! Work with your Golf Professional for more tips and drills on alignment and you will be amazed at how your ball obeys your command to go straight.

Divots

If you take a divot during your swing, including your practice swing, it's okay. In fact, it's quite a good thing, especially with an iron. Taking a divot means you are getting under and through the ball. Just be sure to replace the divot if you live in a growing zone where the divot will re-root itself. Otherwise, take a scoop of ground repair material, usually a mixture of grass seed, fertilizer and soil, located in a container on your motorized golf cart. Spread it over the damaged area, making sure to level it. There may be a bucket with a cover on the tee box area that you can use for divots made on the tee area. Some courses use a different seed mixture for the tee areas. If you aren't sure, just ask in the Pro Shop.

Golfers take this routine seriously because it helps to keep a course in top playing condition. You will understand this completely the day your well-struck ball comes to rest in a deep, ugly, dried-out, unrepaired divot. Sadly, if your ball rolls into a divot during a round, you may not take relief. You must play the ball where it lies. This is one of the tragedies in golf, otherwise referred to as "the rub of the green". It's those spirit-breaking events that might cost you strokes if your club does not make good contact with the ball. You must "play the ball as it lies," otherwise known as "playing the ball down". This is the way the Professionals play and the way you will play once you are ready to play in organized events. On the other hand, there are Winter rules which are most often "local rules" that allow a player to "play the ball up" which lets you move the ball slightly to get a better lie in your fairway. There is also "Lift, Clean and Place" which is allowed by the Green Committee or Pro Shop on a day when a casual round of golf is played after heavy rain and the course might be wet but playable. If your ball is muddy after rolling down the fairway, you may mark your ball where it lies, pick it up, clean it with a towel and place it back exactly where it was, just as you would on the green.

As a *new* golfer, give yourself every opportunity to enjoy your time on the golf course. Move your ball out of the divot and even though you did not create it, fill it. Your course will stay beautiful thanks to your thoughtfulness.

Keep your cool. We don't make a living playing golf.

As my friend, Susan Bond-Philo, PGA, always says, "If you are a polite and considerate person off the course, then you should be a polite and considerate person on the course." Every so often, you may come across a person who is calm and collected in the club house, but is a complete maniac on the course. My position on regular displays of temper is this: if you're not a Professional Golfer, which means practicing long hours every day, hitting the gym for a few hours, having trainers, coaches and nutritionists at your disposal on a daily basis and are playing in tournaments all around the world for millions of dollars, then you have no valid reason to become upset by a bad shot. "Mistakes are part of the game. It's how well you recover from them, that's the mark of a great player." Words of wisdom from Alice Cooper. Yes, even heavy metal rock stars appreciate the art of self-discipline on the golf course.

In our professional lives, we are required to make tactical decisions, develop strategies, use the tools and resources that are available to us and adapt to ever-changing market conditions. That describes what we also have to do on the golf course. We have to make tactical decisions like choosing a target, we have to develop strategies like deciding whether to go over the water or layup. We have to use the tools that are available to us, like choosing a hybrid or an iron for a shot out of deep rough instead of a fairway wood. We have to adapt to ever-changing course conditions like wind, temperature and rain.

When I compete, and sadly, it isn't all that often anymore, my mantra immediately after a bad shot is this, "What is my target? What is my goal?" I do not give myself very much time to fume, but I know there is anger perched on my shoulder. I will try to let it float away. The moment has passed, and the mistake has occurred. What do I need to do right now to get back into play and save strokes? Fuming won't get me through the hole, focusing will.

155

Despite our best efforts at self-control, sometimes we just need to blow off some steam. Maybe you mutter a few words of encouragement to yourself or take a long drink of water. I would much rather you learn to speak nicely to yourself than to berate yourself.

Playing Your First Shot

I hope your drives always go down the middle of the fairway. But, if your tee shot clearly goes "out-of-bounds", you have some work to do. "OB" is defined by a white line, white stakes, or other out-of-bounds markers like property line fences or a stone wall. The penalty you will incur is called "stroke and distance." Announce that you will play a second ball, step out of the tee box and let the other players tee off. After the other players in your group have hit, return to the tee box and hit. Be sure to announce the brand of ball you are now playing. After you hit, you will be lying 3. One stroke for the drive, one penalty stroke for going OB and the stroke you just took to get back into play.

What should you do if you think your first ball might be playable "inbounds", but you can't see it to be certain? In this case, you will hit what is called a "provisional ball." This is a good time to use a golf ball with a different mark on it. So if you put your initials on your golf balls as your "special" mark, draw a circle around your initials, so that if it also slices to the right, you will be able to distinguish it from your first ball. Why? Suppose when you arrive at the location where you think your golf balls landed, you find one ball playable and the other one OB. How will you be able to tell which is your first ball and which is the second ball if you have used the same special mark for both balls?

If your first shot is in fact OB and your second shot is playable, meaning it is in-bounds either on the fairway or in the rough, you will be lying three: one stroke for the first swing, a penalty stroke for going out-of-bounds, and the third stroke that puts you back into play. "Stroke and distance" can also now be a two-stroke penalty if your golf club opts for this local rule. For example, if you hit your ball OB from anywhere other than the tee box, you may bring your ball back into play by dropping it on the edge of the fairway where the ball went OB, no closer to the hole, and hit from there with a 2-stroke penalty. No need to take the long walk backwards.

Don't forget to pick up your "OB" ball (if you can find it quickly) and put it in your pocket. The Official Rules say you have 3 minutes to search for a ball, but everyone really wishes you would only take one or two minutes and then move on. If that ball has seen a lot of combat, let it stay OB. Arrivederci.

Let's further discuss the term "out-of-bounds" for a moment. To be considered "OB", your ball has to be *completely* on the other side of the painted white line or the imaginary line created by the white stakes. A ball that rests with any part of it on the line is considered to be in-bounds and completely playable. You may take your stance outside the line in order to hit your ball if it is lying on the line without penalty.

Once you have reached the area you believe your first ball to be in (remember you have no more than 3 minutes to search for your ball) and you find it "playable," you may pick up your "provisional" ball without penalty. However, if you find the first ball and it is out-of-bounds, or you can't find it at all, return to your "provisional ball", where you will lie 3, having taken the stroke and distance penalty.

Now you see why it's a good idea to carry an extra ball in your pocket in the event your drive, or any other shot, goes out-of-bounds. It lets you get right back into play without having to walk back to your cart or bag, thus saving time. Carrying a second ball also comes in handy on the fairway if you get into trouble with Penalty Areas filled with water.

Beginners

You might not be hitting from the tee box when you start out. You might be happier teeing off from the 150-yard marker. In fact, you should tee your ball up anywhere on the fairway until you get better at making solid contact with the ball. You might like teeing off with a 7-iron. Who cares? Make your time on the course fun and easy until you are ready for yet another bite of the 800 lb elephant.

Tee Box Etiquette

Don't stand directly behind or even the tiniest bit in front of someone teeing off. In fact, stay completely out of the player's peripheral vision preferably so that his or her back is to you.

Don't talk, whisper, or move around while someone is setting up to tee off. This is not the time to open a bag of chips or pop the tab on a can of Arnold Palmer. It is very distracting. Golfers are good sports but can be unforgiving when they feel someone has interfered with a shot, particularly if it costs them a stroke or results in a poor hit. You will most certainly get the "stink eye" from that player. You need to pay attention when members of your group are teeing off.

Learn to keep an eye on the shots of the people in your foursome. If it looks like it's going in the rough or out-of-bounds, find a tree, bush or rock to visually mark the spot where the ball landed. It will help the player find it faster and keep the pace of play moving smoothly. If it looks like it will land too close to players on another fairway or anywhere on the course, don't hesitate to yell "Fore!". These are just some of the ways we learn to be a good sport and considerate golfer. You will appreciate this warning better once you have heard the "whoosh" of a golf ball flying past you. It is unusual but it can happen.

Resist the urge to congratulate someone on a good shot until the ball hits the ground. I've seen hundreds of shots that looked great off the tee, only to be beaten down by the wind and land short of the target or fade in mid-flight and drop into a bunker or disappear into the rough.

If some of the players in your group are using the middle or back tees, and you are using the forward tees, it is a good policy to go to the back tees first. You should never be in front of someone hitting, plus you can help to track their tee shots. Only after they have hit should you go to your tee box. As courteous golfers, they will wait quietly while you set up on your tee and should help you to track your drive as well.

On a busy day, you may have to wait for the group ahead to move out of your range before you can hit. During this time, many players like to take practice swings. If you are one who enjoys this, please make sure you do so away from the people in your group. During a charity outing last summer, I played with a woman who stood in front of us to take a practice swing. I explained to her that it was very easy to contact a stone or a clump of dirt and fling it into the faces of innocent bystanders. I have also seen club heads come off for no apparent reason (Metal fatigue? Thrown too often?) and go flying into the distance. I am sure she didn't realize how uncomfortable we felt and how dangerous her actions actually were.

A better use of your time is to take a look around the fairway and fill any nearby divots and pick up any debris that can sometimes fly out of a cart unnoticed by the driver or passenger. These small acts help to keep your course in top shape.

Respect the Quiet

We know to be quiet on the tee box and putting green. We also know there is noise on the course like birds chirping and frogs croaking. Our golf minds will eventually process that as golf course background noise. Then there is the noise of someone in your group opening a snack box or clanging clubs in her bag while pulling out a club, or the booming voice of the player in the foursome near the water that suddenly makes you feel like you are hearing fingernails dragged down the blackboard. Try to be mindful of any noise distractions you might unwittingly cause during a round, especially when members of your group are hitting.

A Little Noise?

I was playing with some friends at the Fort Lauderdale Country Club one lovely day a few years ago. We were on the 5th hole and I was hitting my second shot to the green. Meanwhile, two of my friends were chatting amiably in the adjacent golf cart, deep in conversation. When they heard my club head strike the ball, they turned to me and began the most sincere apology I have ever heard. I waved it off and said, "Don't worry about it. Let me tell you about Woodland Golf Club, where I play up north." I went on the tell them that the MBTA public transportation trains rumble past the 1st hole green and clang along the 12th hole fairway. There is a busy hospital on Route 16 just across the street from the 8th and 10th hole greens. Every member or guest who has played there has heard the wail of an Ambulance siren in his or her backswing. The Boston Marathon runners and cheering fans take over Route 16 on that exciting day. There are helicopters hovering over the course for hours as they send reports of the race to people watching or listening at home. Woodland golfers hear all of it. (And love it! Boston Strong Forevah.) On the 5th hole green, you can see a snippet of

Route 128 which is 8 lanes of highway filled with tractor-trailers, motorcycles and the occasional horn or screeching brakes, topped off by some really crazy drivers. On occasion, a medivac helicopter will land on the 18th fairway, quickly responding to the Hospital's call to rush a patient to Mass General Hospital. That makes it a little difficult to "play through".

"So don't worry. I never heard a thing.", I said. We all had a good laugh as we continued on our way. By the way, FLCC is very quiet with no homes on the 36 hole property. Once in a while, you might hear a little something from the Florida Turnpike on one of the 36 holes.

Penalty Areas

There you stand on the Par 3 tee with a pond about 75 yards away. Funny thing about bodies of water, they can act like magnets, pulling our golf balls into their murky depths for no apparent reason. Sure enough, your tee shot lands in the middle of the pond and suffers a soggy death. You cannot hit a provisional ball, because your ball is not potentially out-of-bounds. You also cannot declare the ball unplayable. It is, instead, in a penalty area. Penalty areas are defined by the USGA as "any sea, lake, pond, river, ditch, surface drainage ditch or other open water". While they may not always contain water, Penalty Areas are always defined by either yellow or red lines painted on the grass or red or yellow markers, driven into the ground. Unlike the white "out-of-bounds" markers, where your ball can be on the line and still playable, the rule with regard to both yellow and red penalty areas is "if it's *on* the line, it's *in* the penalty area." Thank you Susan Bond-Philo for making this distinction still memorable even after 30 years.

Penalty areas can be located anywhere from off the tee, along the fairway, and in front of the green. Some of them might even be behind the green. Here's how to get your ball back into play.

Yellow Penalty Area

1. You may play the ball where it lies in the water (if it is playable) without penalty. Shoes off, check for snakes and alligators and away you go. You may take a practice swing and ground your club, but you may not improve the swing path by tamping down the area behind the ball. You may also remove loose impediment.

2. If your ball goes in the Penalty Area off the tee, proceed to the designated drop area. Most often, it is a white circle marked "Drop Area". I call it "The Circle of Shame". Now you can, too. You will hit from there. You may not use a tee in the drop area. Add a one stroke penalty plus the stroke that gets you back into play.

3) Stroke and distance. Play from the area from where you just hit. One stroke penalty.

4) Back-on-the-line: Drop a ball within one club length to either side of a straight line from the hole through the point where your ball last crossed the edge of the penalty area, going back as far as necessary. One stroke penalty.

Red Penalty Area

You have all the options listed above plus Lateral Relief.

1. Lateral Relief: Drop a ball within a two-club-length relief area measured from where your ball last crossed the edge of the penalty area, and no closer to the hole than that point. One stroke penalty.

Failure to employ any of these rules results in a two-stroke penalty in Stroke Play and Loss of Hole in Match Play.

Author's Note

Blah, blah, blah. Yada Yada Yada. No doubt, this is what you are feeling right now. Give learning the rules some time. In fact, take all the time you need. Once you get a little better and start playing more, this will all become easy to digest. Until then, don't stress. Put another ball in play and whack it again.

Dropping a Ball

You've now read the term "drop a ball" several times. Here's how to do it properly: stand with knees slightly bent, face the flag stick, drop your hand to the side of one knee and then drop the ball. If your dropped ball rolls closer to the hole or rolls back into the area from which you seek relief, you must drop it again. If it happens a third time, you may place the ball where it hit the ground before it rolled forward. (Or see Author's Note above.)

Bunkers

There is one more area we need to cover as we make our way down the fairway, and that's the bunker, also referred to as a "trap" or "sand trap." In the bunker, you may remove man-made obstructions like paper, bottle caps, cigarette butts, and similar objects, including the rake. If your ball moves while removing a movable obstruction, you may simply replace your ball, penalty-free.

You may also remove loose impediments like leaves, rocks, twigs, or other things made by nature. Just make sure your ball does not move while doing this. If it does, in this case, you will suffer a one-stroke penalty. You may not ground your club before you hit the ball in a bunker. If you do, add two strokes to your score. The grass that borders the bunker is not considered part of the bunker, and therefore a club may be grounded in the grass should you elect to take a practice swing outside of the bunker.

Your ball might be plugged into the high side of a bunker. In golf lingo, you have a "fried egg". Getting out is a difficult shot for even good golfers.

The good news is, unlike being in a Penalty Area, you may declare your ball "unplayable" in a bunker. In this case, you have two options to get back into play.

1) Drop the ball within two club lengths, no closer to the hole, but still in the bunker. One stroke penalty.

2) If you are willing to take two strokes, you can move out of the bunker. Go back as far as necessary on an imaginary line to take relief. If you really, really hate the sand, and you don't mind giving up two strokes, I say why not?

Beginning golfers should take a couple of swipes at the ball and then use a well-executed "hand wedge". Go ahead, pick up your ball and toss it onto the green. Don't give up, just spend some time with your Instructor in the practice bunker.

Your ball may come to rest in casual water in a bunker which entitles you to penalty-free relief, no closer to the hole, but still remaining in the bunker. Relief means you must drop the ball, not place it.

Some other things you'll want to know about being in a bunker have to do with the rake. First, the rake is a movable obstruction. If your ball moves while you're moving the rake, you can replace your ball without penalty. Should your ball come to rest on the rake, you may pick up your ball, move the rake, then drop your ball as close to its original position as possible, without penalty. When entering the bunker, always enter from the low side, it's easier than trying to slide down a deep, sandy slope. Take the rake with you to save time. You will want to carefully rake the bunker *after* your fabulous shot to the green.

You may take some clubs into the bunker with you and you can even lean on a club going into the bunker to help with balance.

Do not drag the rake through the sand or rake any part of the bunker near your ball before you hit your shot. It could be construed as checking the density of the sand and will cost you two strokes in stroke/medal play and loss of the hole in match play. Once you have hit your shot (remember, you can take a practice swing outside of the bunker), rake the sand smooth and either replace the rake in the bunker with the teeth down or off to the side of the bunker. The Golf Club Green Committee decides how they want players to leave the rakes. Some Clubs even have the rakes on the carts, although if you are not used to that, don't be surprised to find quite a few forgotten rakes during your round. Well, I couldn't tell you this had I never been guilty of the aforementioned memory lapse. You figure it out pretty fast when you land in the next bunker and you don't have a rake handy.

Unplayable Lie

Suppose a shot on your way from the tee to the green causes your ball to roll under a bush, fall between some large rocks, or come to rest against a tree or fence presenting you with a situation in which you cannot take a swing at the ball. You have an unplayable lie. Taking a one stroke penalty, you have three choices to get back into play:

1)   Drop your ball within two club lengths, no closer to the hole, which will usually solve the problem. One stroke penalty.
2)   Return to the spot you originally hit from, taking the stroke and distance penalty. One stroke penalty.
3)   Drop your ball as far back as you like from the point it currently lies, keeping that point between you and the hole. One stroke penalty.

Whichever solution you select, remember to count the stroke that got you there, add the penalty stroke, and then count the stroke that gets you back into play from your new location. The penalty for not following one of these three options is loss of hole in match play or a two stroke penalty in stroke/medal play.

Fahgeddaboudit

The picture you will see after this little anecdote was caught on my cell phone camera during a round of golf with my husband, Nick. This was the miserable result of his errant drive and the most undeniable unplayable lie you could ever see. Now my sweet husband is a brilliant business man and his skills as a leader and negotiator are formidable but fair. His skills as a golfer….not so much. With two artificial knees and debilitating back problems, his enjoyment of a round of golf was fading.

Therefore, I invented "Nickie Golf". When we play Nickie Golf, we both hit from the Forward tees. Any of his drives that go in the rough get picked up (by me) and dropped next to my drive. Balls that he hits into a bunker get the same treatment. With the red flag on his golf cart, he can drive anywhere and park a little closer to the green. There is no pressure to play the way he used to (trust me, I don't play the way I used to, either) and now, with Nickie Golf, we are able to enjoy many rounds together as we navigate "The Back Nine" of our lives. We get a little sun, we sip on a High Noon and sometimes we even play a little music.

I share this with you because a big part of golf, of being a golfer and following a golfer's lifestyle, is not just about competing or following all the rules, it's about compassion, companionship and camaraderie. So now you have Cheryl's 3 Cs in addition to Kathy Hart Woods' 3 Cs.

Penalty-free Relief

Assuming you are feeling a bit tired of reading about penalties, this is a good time to tell you about penalty-free relief. (Maybe this is also a good time to freshen your cocktail.)

If your ball comes to rest in a puddle in the middle of the fairway, that is called casual water. Casual water is defined as any water that is not on the course 365 days a year. For example, a recent heavy rain has left a big puddle in the middle of the fairway and your ball has rolled into it. You are entitled to penalty-free relief which means you may select the closest point of relief. That is the spot where you can comfortably stand to address the ball without standing in water, plus one club length, no nearer the hole. Here is how you do it. Once you've found the first dry spot behind the puddle, where you can stand comfortably in the address position without drawing water, insert a tee where your ball would be hit. Lay your longest club, which is your driver, on the ground with one end touching the tee you just inserted into the ground, then put another tee at the other end of the driver, then pick up your club. The space between the two tees is the "area of relief." Make sure you don't move your ball closer to the hole. Bend your knees, face the flag stick, hold your arm out at knee height, and drop the ball between the tees to put it back into play. When you are playing a casual round, it's acceptable to eyeball the area, but when you are in a tournament, you should know how to do this.

If you are taking relief from casual water in a bunker, your ball must stay in the bunker. You will drop your ball with your knees bent and hand by your knees. If your ball rolls back into the water, you may drop it one more time. If you get the same results, you may place your ball in the bunker.

This same procedure holds true for "ground under repair." The Green Keeper will paint a white circle around the area or have a "ground under repair" sign with the area roped off. If it isn't marked, you must play the ball where it lies, no matter how badly the ground is damaged. There's that "rub of the green" again.

You also get penalty-free relief if your ball comes to rest in a hole made by burrowing animals or the Superintendent (digging a hole to repair a broken sprinkler head), or if it comes to rest on the cart path or service road. You also get relief if your ball comes to rest on a pile of grass or other debris intended for removal by the grounds crew.

If you have to stand on the cart path or service road in order to hit the ball, you have the option to take relief in this case as well. If you like the lie of your ball, simply proceed to hit it. However, please keep in mind that when you opt to take relief, it must be full relief. For example, if you have a good lie after you drop the ball, but you still would be standing on the cart path to hit, that is not full relief. You must drop the ball again. Be sure to always take relief properly. Lots of unpleasant encounters have occurred during Member-Member events when proper relief is not taken. Believe me, the discussion can run on for days.

Finally, you get relief (one club length, no closer to the hole) when your ball lands on a green other than the green of the hole you are playing. Remove your ball from the green, use your longest club, placing a tee in the ground at each end, and drop the ball between the tees, no closer to the hole you are playing.

In summary, relief without a penalty is one club length no closer to the hole. Relief with a penalty is two club lengths no closer to the hole.

Continuing Down the Fairway

We have now covered the toughest rules, applying to those unfortunate events that begin on the tee and can follow us along the fairway, into penalty areas or bunkers, and continue to haunt and punish us even when we reach the relative safety of the green.

As you continue along your merry way to becoming a golfer, at some point you will feel ready for some friendly competition. Don't worry, these events have flights whereby players are grouped by handicap. The ladies with whom you will play all have similar handicaps to yours.

During this friendly competition, you will need to keep an accurate count of how many strokes you have taken. When you become a seasoned golfer, not only must you be able to quickly and accurately report *your* score for a hole, but you must also be able to track the score of your opponent. A word of caution here: it can get ~~messy, confusing~~ …..err…. a tiny bit testy on occasion. So now that you know how to count how many strokes have been taken, here is what you can do when you need to defend your score *and* recite the score of your opponent.

Your opponent, Delores, will tell you she had a 7 on a Par 4 with two handicap strokes on her scorecard. You will want to politely and calmly say something like, "Well, Delores, let's recap the hole together. Your drive was one, your whiff on the fairway was two, your worm burner was three, your shot into the water was four, add one for the penalty which makes five and then your shot into the bunker comes to six, the two shots required to get out of the bunker comes to eight and your three putts brings us to a total of eleven, for a net score of nine."

Now I know this must sound ridiculous, and yes, I am poking a little fun at poor, fictitious Delores. But compare knowing how to keep track of your score and one other player to how you examine the bill before you plunk down your American Express card after an expensive dinner for four at a fine restaurant. You certainly are going to do a quick scan of all the items that were ordered at the restaurant that night. You have to be sure the numbers add up, and that an $800 check is not a $1,200 check before you sign the bill.

Over time, you will develop the habit of tracking your strokes taken and as you improve and become more "golf game aware", you will easily be able to count the strokes of others. One of the many things that causes slow play is the golfer who stands on the green and looks back at the hole she just played, trying to count her strokes. Another good habit to develop is the ability to follow the direction of the ball when members of your foursome hit. When we don't pay attention, more time is wasted looking for balls, which backs up the course. You can do your part to keep play moving, especially when riding, by thinking about your next shot before you even get to your ball. Find a distance marker en route and have an idea of which clubs you might need. If your cart partner's ball is on the other side of the fairway, grab a couple of clubs and head for your ball on foot, suggesting she drive to her ball. Watching an experienced foursome of golfers who play together often is a thing of beauty. Everyone knows what to do to keep things moving along.

If your course doesn't have GPS in the carts, use your hand-held range finder to check your distance to the flag stick. As you move along the fairway, take a moment to consider where members of your group are, who is away and play ready golf whenever you can. Ready golf simply means whoever is ready to hit, providing it is safe to do so, should hit.

If your shot has landed in the another fairway, and the foursome playing that fairway is making its way to where your ball landed, they have the right of way. This is a tricky situation to explain, but simply stated, you have no right to enter their fairway until that group has passed. Now, there are times when the approaching foursome will give you a wave to go ahead and hit. In the absence of any communication from them, you must yield.

171

Unless the course states that you may play "winter rules," which means you may take a preferred lie (pertaining to balls in your fairway only), you must "play the ball down," which means you must play it where it lies. If a player improves her lie or touches her ball before reaching the green when winter rules are not in effect, it is a two stroke penalty. When winter rules are in effect, you may mark your ball, pick it up, clean it, and place it (do not drop it) near the marker, no closer to the hole. This action is commonly referred to as "lift, clean, and place."

Although the *USGA Official Rules* book does not recognize winter rules or preferred lies under any circumstances, some courses allow it to protect the course, especially if there is new grass or a recent heavy rain has made the fairways wet and muddy.

Damaged Ball

If your ball becomes damaged during the course of a hole either by hitting a rock, tree, or cart path, you may replace it without penalty because it is unfit for play. The time to do this is during the hole in which it becomes unfit or between holes. You may not put a different ball down if you are worried, for example, that your next shot won't clear the water. Keep in mind that you must 1) announce in advance to your opponent or fellow competitor that you intend to lift your ball to examine it and 2) mark the position of the ball before it is lifted. Failure to do either is a one stroke penalty.

Other Faux Pas and Penalties

It's always a good policy to identify your ball before you hit. That's why having your own symbol drawn on your ball is so important. Sometimes we can become distracted or forget where our ball is, especially if we've been helping another player to look for a lost ball. It is not uncommon then, for a player to return to a ball on the fairway and hit it, thinking it is her ball, only to discover moments later that it was not her ball.

In Match Play, you will lose the hole. In Stroke Play, it is a two stroke penalty. If the mistake is not rectified before teeing off on the next hole, or if you leave the green on the final hole without rectifying the error, you are subject to disqualification in Stroke Play. The only penalty-free exception to this rule is if you play another person's ball in a penalty area. Just return the player's ball to the spot where you hit it, find your ball, and continue playing. If someone hits your ball, which was not in a penalty area, she has the unpleasant task of adding two penalty strokes to her scorecard. Experienced golfers will immediately admit their mistakes. If they don't, you may politely notify that person of the two stroke penalty. You may then place your ball as close as possible to its original spot. The person who hit your ball now must find her ball and play it. If she cannot find it, it is considered "lost" and she must use the stroke and distance penalty and go back to where she last hit from with an additional one stroke penalty. Penalty strokes can add up quickly from careless mistakes.

Now you are beginning to appreciate the importance of applying a special symbol to your ball. This habit of marking your ball with your unique symbol comes into focus again, when, for example, you and another player are playing on parallel fairways and you both hit in the rough while playing the same brand of ball. If neither of you can positively identify your golf ball, then both balls would be considered lost for lack of proper identification. This is a very frustrating way to have unwanted strokes added to your scorecard. What happens next? You will employ our old friend, Stoke and Distance, with a one stroke penalty.

It is never a good idea to ask someone what club she used on a shot if she's your opponent. That question earns you a one stroke penalty in Stroke play and loss of the hole in Match play. In fact, the distance you hit your 9-iron could be 20 yards shorter than another player with more strength or 20 yards further than a newer player. Furthermore, the club you might need for a 130-yard shot from the fairway may not be the club you'll need to cover the same distance from the rough. The best advice is to find out at the driving range what you get for distance from each club and see how that works on the course. Get to know *your* game. There are exceptions to this suggestion, especially when you are playing in a scramble or with a partner. It may be helpful to your teammate(s) to let them know which club you selected for the shot so they can better gauge what might work for them.

Don't ever be afraid to "take more club" on a shot. When Susan Bond-Philo was teaching me she told me that most amateur golfers tend to under-club. She said when I start flying the ball over the green, we will start working on that. All these years later, I still don't fly the green.

Loose Impediments and Immovable Obstructions

Sometimes a leaf, twig, or fallen branch will interfere with your ability to address the ball. You may move the "impediments" as long as you do not cause the ball to move. If you cause the ball to move, it is a one stroke penalty. You must replace your ball as close as possible to the spot from which it was moved. If your ball is in the rough in tall grass, you may not pat down the grass behind the ball to improve the swing path. You may not break or bend branches from trees to improve your swing path. Doing so earns you a loss of hole in Match Play and a 2-stroke penalty in Stroke Play.

If your ball comes to rest near the red or yellow stakes defining penalty areas, a cart sign, or the stakes that hold a length of chain or rope near the green to deter motorized carts from going too close to the green, you may move these objects, take your shot, and then replace them.

However, if your ball comes to rest against a white out-of-bounds stake or the fence or stone wall that defines out-of-bounds, you may not move these stakes. You do not get relief because out-of-bounds markers are considered an integral part of the course. What you have then is an unplayable lie. Taking a one stroke penalty, you may drop the ball two club lengths, no closer to the hole, or take one of the two other unplayable lie options discussed earlier.

An immovable obstruction is any man-made/artificial object on the course including buildings, roads, ball washers, benches, fences, signs, and white stakes that indicate out-of-bounds. The objective of the free drop, one club length, no nearer the hole, is to improve your stance and allow you to swing freely. If the obstruction is still in your target line, you must accept your fate and accept a shorter distance shot or move laterally. That's why you want to be able to hit a good "bump and run" shot. It will help you to get back into play.

Don't Hesitate to Pick Up

If you are having the hole from hell and are at double-par halfway down the fairway, pick up your ball and put it in your pocket. By picking up, you are doing yourself a favor by taking a little time to calm down. You can try again at the next hole. You are also doing the people in your foursome a favor by allowing them to move along, not to mention the foursome behind you, who will be singing your praises as a courteous player. Try to keep in mind that golf is just a form of entertainment for us. I have a much higher opinion of someone who has her ball in her pocket, having given the hole her best shot, than the duffer who stubbornly insists on just one more shot, while we all have to stand aside for the next worm burner.

Equitable Stroke Control lets you save some face. You can adjust your score before you post it on your mobile GHIN app or the GHIN site. Don't moan and groan about a big number on a hole, or several holes or the entire round. Just do it and be done with it. Remember what Kathy Hart Wood said and remain neutral about numbers.

You will find the Equitable Stroke Control Table in Chapter 9.

Driving the Golf Cart

Good manners as a cart driver are just as important as good manners as a golfer. Observe the rules for the use of carts at the club where you are playing. If the club wants you to keep the cart on the path at all times, please do so. To speed play, develop the habit of taking extra clubs from your bag, along with your range finder, when you head for your ball. Using a cart does not mean you have to ride to every shot, especially as you approach the green. In fact, searching for a lost ball on foot can be more efficient than riding through the woods or the rough in the cart. Encourage your partner to take the cart to her ball if she is across the fairway. You can walk to the cart after taking your shot. These habits all contribute to maintaining the pace of play.

Make sure your cart partner is completely seated before you drive off to the next hole. Also, make sure the clubs your cart partner is selecting from her golf bag are completely out of the bag before you drive away. If you're being bounced around by an inconsiderate cart driver, don't hesitate to speak up. If it's upsetting you, then it's affecting your game. You are not in the Indy 500 and golf carts are not toys. I have a plate and four screws in my cervical spine and bulging disks in my lumbar spine. Guess who drives the cart? Moi.

When a course asks you to "observe the 90-degree rule" they are telling you it is permissible to take the carts on the fairway, but they want you to drive in the rough until you reach your ball. When you take the cart onto the fairway, turn onto the fairway at a 90-degree angle.

Always put the parking brake on, especially if you are playing a hilly course, and turn the wheels such that if the brake accidentally releases, the cart will roll to a safe place and not into people. If a parked cart does take off, do not chase it. It is only equipment. Make sure no one is in its path and let it come to rest on its own. Better a damaged cart than an injured player.

Be aware of where other players are on the course as you motor by in your cart. Don't drive up to the next tee if the foursome on it is preparing to tee off. Be mindful of putting the cart into reverse when people are putting or teeing off nearby. The beep beep beep back-up warning sound that carts make while in reverse could disturb someone's concentration. More recently, some golfers enjoy music while they golf. If you are playing music in your cart, please be mindful of the volume so as to not disturb those who prefer the quiet of the golf course. It's good cart management to park the cart near that side of the green you will exit after holing out which gets you to the next tee via the shortest route. If your cart partner is on the green, and you are not, grab your putter and whatever wedges you want, and walk back to your ball. Have her take the cart to park it green side. Drive the cart as you would an automobile. By that I mean don't operate the cart from the passenger side.

You'd be surprised how easily a golf cart can get away from you, resulting in accidents that cause serious injury to the driver, other players, or expensive damage to the cart.

Why yes, that's me as a new golfer sometime in the early 90s, driving the golf cart, ahem, into the first hole sign at the prestigious Copperhead Course at Innisbrook, located in Palm Harbor, FL. Fortunately, no one was injured. (Aside from my ego.) The sign remained intact. The cart roof support bar had a slight bend, as you can clearly see. My girlfriend captured this embarrassing moment on her camera. I am one of those people who laughs when something like this happens. No one was injured. The damage to the cart was nominal. Someone from the Pro Shop came out. He didn't have far to walk since we were at the first tee. As soon as we all assured him there were no bodily injuries, he was bent over laughing, too. They could not have been more gracious.

I have used this photo in countless presentations and it gives me great pleasure to see everyone laugh. This is a prop to display before any golf clinic you may host for your colleagues because it takes the pressure away. It shows we are all just human and bound to make mistakes. Now, you might be wondering exactly how this happened.

"Well, Your Honor, I was eating a sandwich, having just completed the first 18 holes. A girl gets hungry out there, you know. I was carelessly driving the cart while gazing to my left to watch my cart partner tee off for our second 18. And that is exactly when the sign jumped out in front of me."

I hope this kind of moment never happens to you. I could write another book just on bloopers and Grille Room tall tales. All kidding aside, please be careful when driving the golf cart. Oh, and if you want to smoke in my cart, please do not exhale.

Lightning: What to Do in an Electrical Storm

Dit Dit da Dit Dit Dit. We interrupt this captivating Rules chapter to bring you a very important announcement.

What can you do in the event of an electrical storm coming your way during your round? Imagine a sultry summer day that is overcast and very humid. You've paid big bucks to play in a charity outing with an executive from the bank you are hoping to sign as your new software client. Your group is on the 13th hole, way out there on the course, far from the club house . Suddenly, you hear thunder in the distance and turn to see some very dark and ominous clouds over your shoulder. Rest assured that the Pro Shop has been monitoring the weather very closely on their radar system. The warning horn (there are several warning horns installed around the golf course) will sound to warn all players to halt play and seek shelter. Please, immediately stop whatever you are doing, leave your golf balls where they lay, and head for the club house or on-course shelter, even if it is the Rest Room, Snack Shack, maintenance building or cart barn. Do not drive to your ball to pick it up. Leave it. Do not finish your putt. Head for shelter right away. A bolt of lightning can travel up to 10 miles in a matter of seconds. If the skies open and the thunder and lightning continue, and you cannot find shelter, here is a list of suggestions to keep you safe until you can get inside.

1)   Head into a dense, wooded area. Avoid isolated trees. They are magnets for a lightning strike.

2)   If you are caught in the open, get on your knees in a tucked position in the lowest spot near you.

3)   Do not use your umbrella and stay away from your golf clubs.

4)   Stay away from the water.

5)   Do not seek refuge in the cart. It is not safe.

The only exception to this directive is if you are playing in a Club Championship, Qualifier or any other "Major" golf event. Once the horn is sounded, you must mark your ball and pick it up. However, you may not proceed to play, even to tap in a 2-inch putt.

Golf courses take electrical storms very seriously and always monitor the weather closely with their in-house radar systems. They will act quickly to call players in when lightning threatens.

Once the storm has passed and it is deemed by the Pro Shop that players can safely return to the course, the horn will sound twice signaling "All clear. Return to play." Then just go back to the hole you were playing and resume play. Hope you wore your waterproof shoes and packed your rain gear that day.

"There was a thunderous crack like cannon fire and suddenly I was lifted a foot and a half off the ground. Damn, I thought to myself, this is a helluva penalty for slow play."

Lee Trevino on being struck by lightning

On the Green

The green is *hallowed* ground. More effort goes into building a green and more money goes into maintaining it than any other part of the course. This is also the place where players probably get into the most trouble in terms of etiquette and rules, so let's review everything you need to know, beginning with etiquette.

Assuming you are driving the cart, observe the course rules about how close a motorized golf cart can come to the green. Usually, a course will paint a line on the grass telling you that you may not cross that line with your motorized cart or have a specially marked stake in the ground which indicates it is time to find that green side parking spot. If the course has not marked it off, a good rule of thumb is to stay at least 30 yards away. If your cart is equipped with GPS, your cart will shut down if you get too close to the green and you will have the noisy task of backing away (beep beep beep) from the area until your cart allows you to drive forward again. You may cross the line with your pull cart or when carrying your bag, but never take these items onto the green. Leave them off to the side.

Park your cart in such a way that when you exit the green, you are ready to head to the next tee. Be sure to leave enough room for another cart or a course maintenance vehicle to get by, if necessary. If you are using a pull cart, leave it as close as possible to the next tee. The goal here is to walk off the green just as soon as your group has holed out and proceed to the next tee without delay. Having to walk back to a cart that was carelessly parked in front of a large green complex slows play for the foursome behind you and is looked upon as inconsiderate and a rookie mistake.

Mark your scorecards only when you are off the green, and out of the way of the group behind you, preferably at the next tee. I am hard-pressed to think of anything more annoying than the player who stands on the green, looks back at the hole we've just completed and begins to add up her score for the hole. Please, try to count your strokes as you hit.

Marking Your Ball on the Green

Once your ball is on the green, mark it no matter where it lies. This gives you an opportunity to pick up your ball and wipe off any dirt or grass on it so your putt will roll smoothly. To properly mark your ball, place your marker behind the ball without touching or moving it. Once the marker is in place, you may pick up your ball. To return your ball to play, place the ball in front of the marker and pick up the marker without moving the ball.

If your ball marker is in someone's line of putt, she may ask you to move your marker to the right or left. Here's how to do it properly. Keeping one end of your putter on the marker, pick an object on the course like a bush or a tree and visually line up the front of your putter head with that object. Remove your marker from its current position at the front of the putter and place the marker at the opposite end of the putter. Once again, you may not move your marker closer to the hole. When it's your turn to putt, don't forget to move your marker back to its original position. I use a decorative metal ball marker and I will turn it over to the dull side if I have to move my ball. That way, I have a reminder to move my marker back to its original position. Finally, if you are the player who asked another player to mark her ball, give her a friendly reminder to move her ball back to its original position. It is a respectful gesture and always appreciated.

Repairing a Ball Mark

Assuming you made a pitch mark on the green when your ball dropped down from that beautifully lofted wedge shot, now is the time to repair it. To do so properly, take your ball mark repair tool or a tee from your pocket and insert it at one end of the indentation, then gently pull the top of the tool toward the center of the "dent". Continue working around the ball mark until the hole is closed. Do not twist or pull up on the tool as this will disturb the grassroots.

Then gently tap down the area with the bottom of your putter so that it is level with the green.

Repairing ball marks keeps the greens smooth and in good condition. An unrepaired indentation dries out, causing the grass to die and leaving players with a bumpy putting surface. A repaired golf ball mark will heal within a matter of hours. An unrepaired ball mark will take weeks to recover.

A good rule of thumb when it comes to ball marks is to fix yours and one other, especially on the Par 3s. They get the most wear and tear from lofted shots.

Here are some things to remember in the "good manners" department when you are on the green.

1. Do not walk on someone's "putt line."

2. Pick up your feet so you do not scuff the green. Even spikeless shoes can damage the greens if players drag their feet while walking.

3) Be careful not to damage the lip of the cup when removing your ball from the hole or when replacing the flag stick. Don't use your putter to dig out your ball. Always use your hand.

4) Repair your ball mark (if you made one) and one more if you see one. This doesn't mean you should spend ten minutes repairing ball marks. Just fix yours and one other if it is easily spotted.

5) If someone has been kind enough to mark your ball for you, be sure to return her ball marker after you hole out.

6) Do not stand behind the hole or in the peripheral vision of the player who is putting.

7) Do not "prowl" the green. We are not on the LPGA Tour. Looking at your putt from every angle is taking more time than necessary. Assess your line as you are walking to your ball, then get your read from behind the ball.

8) Putt it out. If you are just a few inches from the hole, tap it in rather than mark it to save time. Just ask, "May I finish?". More than likely, your fellow players will either give you the putt or agree to let you tap it in. The only time you are not able to do this is in any form of competition that requires all players in the field to hole the ball.

If your friends "give you the putt", remember to count the stroke. Also, when you are given a putt, please pick up your ball.

9) Be very quiet and still while others are putting.

10) If your ball stops on the very edge of the hole, it has 10 seconds to drop in. You may not blow on it, stamp your feet around it or influence it in any way. If it has not dropped into the hole after 10 seconds, you may tap it in and count the stroke.

The Putt Line

What is the "putt line?" It's an imaginary line that runs from the location of a player's ball to the cup, taking into account the "break," or undulation of the green. It is rarely a straight line, so step carefully. If you cannot see the other three markers, don't hesitate to ask, "Where are you marked?", to avoid stepping on someone's line. Some players don't mind if you step on their putt line, and will tell you not to worry about it. Others will hold you responsible if they miss a putt because you stepped on their putt line and will let you know in no uncertain terms. It is always better to be overly cautious on this particular point, especially if you're playing with people you do not know well.

You may pick up twigs, brush away sand and repair ball marks and scuff marks in your putt line without penalty.

The Flag Stick: Help or Hindrance

Also referred to as the "Pin", there was a lot of fuss over it before the 2019 Rules change and particularly during Covid. In the "old days," the Flag Stick could be either tended by a caddy or a player or it was removed when a player was putting. If the player's ball hit the flag stick while putting, there was a penalty.

Today, tending the pin has gone by the wayside. As Covid cases were decreasing, and some outdoor activity returned, no one wanted to touch the flag stick because it would be handled by so many players. Under the new rule, a player may either leave the flag stick in when putting or have it removed. You will have to decide if leaving the flag stick in the hole will help or hinder your putt. I have had good and bad experiences with it, so only your own playing experience will give you your answer.

It's common courtesy for the first person to hole out (sink the putt) to replace the flag stick after everyone has holed out. Be careful not to damage the area around the cup when replacing the flag stick. The lip of the cup, like everything on the green, is very carefully maintained by the grounds crew. No one wants to putt into a damaged cup. An uneven rim could prevent a good putt from dropping into the hole.

Just as you would on the tee, do not stand too close to or in the peripheral vision of someone who's putting. Do not stand directly behind the cup. During this time you should stand still and not talk. If a player's ball comes to rest just a few inches from the cup, and you are playing a casual round, you can tell her "It's good." and let her pick it up. The stroke will have to be counted, but you are being courteous by saving her a two or three-inch putt. If you are playing in a tournament, everyone must hole out because you are playing against the field. In casual play, when someone tells you your putt is "good" you should thank her and pick up your ball right away. It is considered rude to putt out after your putt has been given to you. While there is no penalty for putting out, it is not good form. Be sure to add the stroke to your score for the hole. For example, if you get to the green in four strokes, your excellent putt stops a breath away from the cup and your group "gives" you the next putt, your score will be six.

Good Green Etiquette

1. Don't walk or stand on anyone's putt line.

2. Don't cast a shadow over the hole or the putt line. Everyone on the green should make sure a shadow is not being cast on a player's line of putt or over the hole.

3. Stand to either side of the hole, never behind it.

Here are some tips to keep in mind when it's your turn to putt:

1) You may remove loose impediments in your line of putt, even if you are off the green. Loose impediments are sand, stones, leaves, insects, etc. You may pick them up or brush them away with your hand or club head. If your ball is moved as a result of clearing loose impediments, just replace it without penalty.

2) If your ball comes to rest at the edge of the cup, it has ten seconds to go into the cup to be considered holed. You may not do anything to force it in. If it does not go in or goes in after ten seconds have passed (a train rumbles by causing the ball to drop in), it is a penalty stroke, otherwise interpreted as the same score you would record if you had tapped the ball in. The same rule applies in match play.

3) If your ball hits another ball while you are putting in match play, there is no penalty. Just replace the ball you hit where it was, and play yours where it lies. However, in stroke play, it's a two stroke penalty. Return the ball you hit to its original position, and play yours where it lies.

5) If you hit an object while putting (for example, someone's club is lying on the green), or a person (specifically, your opponent or the caddy) in match play, just play your ball as it lies, penalty-free. Or you may elect to replay the stroke as long as no other players have taken a stroke. In stroke play, there is no penalty, but you must count the stroke and play your ball where it lies.

When everyone has holed out, take a quick look around the green to check if anyone has left a club behind. Having done that, it is time to head to the next tee. Remember to mark your scorecard on your way to the next tee, not in the cart by the green.

Committing the Rules to Memory

It may take a few readings before this chapter makes sense, especially if you are just starting to play. Maybe you will read through it, maybe you will read it at a later date. Let me offer an old saying about how people learn, "I hear and I forget, I see and I remember, I do and I understand."

If you are told about a certain rule, you will probably soon forget it. If you take the time to read about a rule or two, you'll most likely remember some of it, and when you are able to apply the rule accurately while playing, then you will understand it.

The best way to learn the rules is to play with people who know the rules, follow them, and are willing to help you learn them either during the course of a round as you ride or walk to your next shot or after the round. If you intend to be taken seriously, you must know a few of the important rules and follow the etiquette. Having a command of this critical part of the game will quickly earn you the admiration and respect of your golfing peers. You can always ask your Golf Professional to explain and even demonstrate a rule. Their willingness to help you learn and enjoy this wonderful game is their chosen profession, and they really do care about your progress.

If you would like a nifty assistant with the rules of golf, visit www.knowyourgolfrules.com

There are 8 credit card size tags on a key chain with a quick synopsis of the new rules printed on both sides. I think this would make a great tee gift for a Guest Day or Opening Day at your golf club or giveaway in a Welcome Bag.

"Luck is not chance, it's Toil.

Fortune's Expensive Smile is Earned."

Emily Dickinson

Chapter 9

The World Handicap System

Why Golf is an Equal Opportunity Sport

The World Handicap System allows for a level playing field for all players, regardless of ability. It is an internationally recognized, consistently and fairly applied system that rates the difficulty of a golf course by assigning each course a "rating" and a "slope."

The course *rating* is based on the score a scratch golfer would shoot for 18 holes on that particular course. A course rating of 72.0 would indicate that a scratch golfer would shoot 72, in other words, even par for 18 holes. With the same consideration, a course that has a 72 rating, a bogey golfer would shoot 90, or 18 strokes over par.

The *slope* is a measure of a course's difficulty for a scratch player compared to players who are not. Determining the rating and slope for a golf course comes from the state golf association. They inspect and analyze every aspect of the course. They measure distances to penalty areas, the size and contours of the greens, the severity of the bunkers and the length of a hole from tee to green. There are probably a few dozen more aspects of each hole taken into consideration. The results are plugged into an algorithm that will generate the Course Rating for a scratch golfer and the bogey rating. A slope rating of 113 represents the lowest degree of difficulty. The highest rating is 155, which is like leaving the Bunny Trail at the Aspen ski resort and going down a Black Diamond trail with one ski and one ski pole. You are going to have the ride of your life.

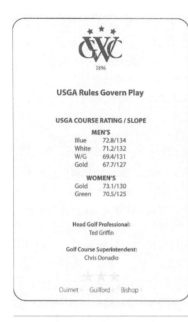

On a scorecard, each tee will have a different slope. For example, the Blue tees on this card have a slope of 134. The White tees are 132 and the forward tees are 125. Same with the rating. The number increases along with the level of difficulty with the Blue tees rated at 72.8 while the Green tees have a rating of 70.5.

A Handicap Index can range from zero (for the "scratch" golfer), to a maximum of 40.4 for women and 36.4 for men. "Scratch" simply means an individual shoots par (usually 72) for 18 holes. Not in my wheelhouse, but it is common for Professional golfers and some gifted amateurs to be a +1, +2 or even more.

How Do You Get a Handicap?

Tell your Golf Professional you would like to get a handicap. Every golf club subscribes to the GHIN (Golf Handicap Index Number) system. There is a modest annual fee join. Private clubs don't charge (trust me, it is folded into your charges somewhere), and usually junior golfers get one at no charge. After you have submitted score cards from at least five 18-hole rounds or ten 9-hole rounds, your average score will be calculated according to the system created by the USGA. That number, taking into account the slope, course rating, and which set of tees you play from, will give you your Handicap Index.

You will then be given a GHIN membership number in the World Handicap System and your handicap will be updated every two weeks. You can download the GHIN app on your phone, laptop or PC. Enter all of your scores (religiously) and follow your progress. You can even look up other players who are in the system. It comes in handy when you want to play a friendly match and need to look up your group's current Index numbers in order to stroke the card fairly.

A player can get a 9-hole or an 18-hole handicap or both. Turn in *all* your scores, including the good, the bad, and the ugly. It's the only way to measure your true handicap. If you are usually scoring in the high 90s and have a score of 110 from a bad round, don't worry. The next round back in the 90s will kick that high score out. The handicap is calculated using your most recent *lowest* scores. In some cases, players must provide their GHIN number to give evidence of playing ability before being allowed to play in state and national tournaments. We don't have to worry about that just yet. Maybe this will never cross our radar screen again, but I like to cover all the bases.

Match vs. Stroke Play

There are two forms of competition in golf. One is Match play, the other is Stroke play. Stroke play is sometimes also called Medal play.

In Match play, you are playing on a hole-by-hole basis. The team or individual who won the most holes during the round wins. In

Match play, the score doesn't determine victory, just the number of holes won. Match play is a great format in which to compete because anything can happen to tip the scale in your favor. For example, let's imagine that you are playing a Match play against another individual. You both tee off; her drive goes right down the middle, but your drive drifts to the right and goes into the rough, but not out of bounds. Upon arriving at your ball, you are delighted to see that you have a clear shot. You hit and your ball lands 80 yards away from the green.

Your opponent then proceeds to top her second shot so that it only advances a few yards. Her third shot, however, lands on the green, but not close to the pin. You then proceed to dump your third shot into the green side bunker. However, a splendid bunker shot places you about three feet from the cup.

Your opponent sends her fourth shot, which is an aggressive putt, way past the cup and rolls off the green and into the rough. Her fifth shot, a chip, skips by the hole and now she is about fifteen feet from the cup. Two more putts are required and she finally holes out with a 7. She had a stroke on that hole, so she finished 7, net 6.

Lying four, you sink your putt, taking the hole with five. Your handicap gives you a stroke on that hole, so you have 5, net 4. Your gross 5 beat her net 6.

Even though your opponent had a good drive and yours went into the rough, even though she was on the green in three while you were in the bunker in three, you still won the hole.

The beauty of Match play is that you can always recover from a bad shot or a couple of bad shots if you stay mentally focused and grind it out. You never know what's going to happen to your opponent. It is easier to win a round "hole by hole" in Match play than to win a round vying for the lowest gross score in Stroke play.

In my own experience with Match play, I just play to the best of my ability, be patient and wait for my opponent to make a mistake.

In Stroke play, the lowest score at the end of the round (counting every bloody, gut-wrenching, God-forsaken stroke) determines the winner. Not for newer golfers or the faint-of-heart, Stroke play is grueling. If your ball goes in the water 4 times on a hole, you have to take your penalty strokes and play the ball until you hole out. I have seen players get up to 21 strokes on a single Par 4 hole. It is sad to see and incredibly upsetting for the player. Better to stand aside and offer no comment while something this tragic is happening. There is nothing you or anyone could say to ease that player's wounded ego and shattered confidence. If I am playing with that person, I will wait a couple of holes and then quietly offer some words of encouragement. While no one coddles the Professionals when they put up a big number, my opponents are also my golf club friends. We are all part of a golf club community. I will always take a moment to be empathetic. Remember I mentioned earlier in the book: no one will remember how you played, but they will remember how you treated them. Kindness is an invaluable qualilty.

Equitable Stroke Control

If you're like me, every now and then, you fall apart on a hole. Your ball has gone OB off the tee and then into the water once or twice, and the possibility of holing out before the sun sets in the West seems remote. Equitable Stroke Control is for those occasions so the "hole from hell" will not artificially elevate your handicap. Equitable Stroke Control sets the maximum number a player can post on any hole depending on the player's course handicap. There isn't a limit on the number of holes you can adjust *after* your round before you post your final adjusted score to your GHIN app.

In USGA lingo, ESC is the downward adjustment of individual hole scores for handicap purposes in order to make handicaps more representative of a player's potential ability. We use ESC only when a player's actual or most likely score exceeds the player's maximum number on the table that follows below.

18-Hole Equitable Stroke Control

Course Handicap	Maximum Number on Any Hole
9 or less	Double Bogey
10 through 19	7
20 through 29	8
30 through 39	9
40 or more	10

9-Hole Equitable Stroke Control

Course Handicap	Maximum Number on Any Hole
4 or less	Double Bogey
5 through 9	7
10 through 14	8
15 through 19	9
20 or more	10

There is one important exception to this rule. If you are playing in a Medal/Stroke play tournament, you cannot pick up your ball. You must record every stroke for the hole, even if it is a big number like 15 on a Par 5, even if you have 6 holes with a 10. If the whole idea isn't nerve-wracking enough, at the first tee, you must give your scorecard to your opponent and she will give you her scorecard. You will be keeping her score and your own. She will be keeping your score and her own. It keeps everything honest. At the end of the round, you must agree on both of your total scores and sign the cards. Then you will turn them in ato the Head Golf Professional who will then post the scores on he Leader Board. You may adjust your score for submission using ESC and then post it on your GHIN app. But your gross score will go up on the Leader Board for all to see. As an aside, should anyone comment about your score who is *not* playing in the competition, just ask them where their name is up there.

You may never, ever play in a Medal/Stroke event. I have done it many times and it gives me considerable anxiety. Or as we say in Italian, I get agita.

Don't trouble yourself with thoughts of Medal/Stroke play for now. Your focus as a new golfer is to have fun and enjoy yourself. Just remember, once you start keeping score, make sure you post your score before midnight of the day you played. Sometimes players might get a friendly e-mail from the Golf Committee reminding them to get that score posted.

Visiting Other Courses

When you play other courses, you can check the Course Handicap Calculator, which you will find on the USGA app. It will help you to adjust your handicap for the round you are about to play. If you are playing in a Member-Guest, no need to worry. Once the host Pro Shop has your GHIN number, they will take care of all the calculations and your scorecard will be stroked appropriately and ready for you on the golf cart. Do not stress about any of this for now. Keep it light and easy. Just go out and have fun. All of this information will still be here for you when you are ready. Unless that is, you decide to use these pages to line your bird cage.

Stroking a Scorecard

Stroking a scorecard is easy. Let's say you're playing with three friends at your club. Imagine that your handicap is 22 and your friends have 13, 18, and 28, respectively. There are two ways to handle this. One way is for the player with the 13 handicap to "host the party". Everyone will play off of her handicap and she plays "at scratch", meaning she does not get any strokes. Or, you all play against Par, which means you all get handicap strokes where appropriate on your scorecard.

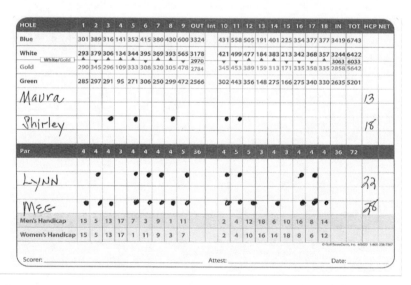

HOLE	1	2	3	4	5	6	7	8	9	OUT	Int	10	11	12	13	14	15	16	17	18	IN	TOT	HCP	NET
Blue	301	389	316	141	352	415	380	430	600	3324		431	558	505	191	401	225	354	377	377	3419	6743		
White	293	379	306	134	344	395	369	393	565	3178		421	499	477	184	383	213	342	368	357	3244	6422		
White/Gold										2970											3063	6033		
Gold	290	345	296	109	333	308	320	305	478	2784		345	453	389	159	313	171	335	358	335	2858	5642		
Green	285	297	291	95	271	306	250	299	472	2566		302	443	356	148	275	166	275	340	330	2635	5201		
Maura																							13	
Shirley		●		●			●					●	●										18	
Par	4	4	3	4	4	4	4	4	5	36		4	5	5	3	4	3	4	4	4	36	72		
Lynn		●		●	●	●		●				●	●					●	●				22	
Meg	●	●	●		●	●	●	●	●			●	●	●		●		●	●	●			28	
Men's Handicap	15	5	13	17	7	3	9	1	11			2	4	12	18	6	10	16	8	14				
Women's Handicap	15	5	13	17	1	11	9	3	7			2	4	10	16	14	18	8	6	12				

Scorer: _____ Attest: _____ Date: _____

Looking at the scorecard above, you'll see that each hole is assigned a handicap number from 1 to 18. The #1 handicap hole is ranked as the most difficult hole on the course and it will always be on the Front Nine, while the #18 handicap hole will be the easiest hole on the course. The #2 handicap hole will be on the

196

Back Nine, the #3 handicap hole will be on the Front Nine, and so it will go back and forth until all 18 holes have a handicap rating.

In the first scenario, the player with the 13 will play at "scratch" getting no strokes because the other ladies will be playing off of her handicap. She will give five strokes to the woman with the 18-handicap (18 minus 5 equals 13), 9 strokes to you (22 minus 13 equals 9), and 15 strokes (28 minus 13 equals 15) to the woman with the 28-handicap.

Place a check mark or a dot on the holes where the three players will "stroke" against the lowest handicap player. Therefore, the player with the 18-handicap will get strokes on handicap holes 1 through 5, the 22-handicap player will get strokes on handicap holes 1 through 9, and the player with the 28-handicap will get strokes on holes 1 through 15. At the end of the round, you will add up both gross and net scores. The net score is just the gross score minus the strokes. Just like our paychecks when the taxes are deducted.

HOLE	1	2	3	4	5	6	7	8	9	OUT	Int	10	11	12	13	14	15	16	17	18	IN	TOT	HCP	NET
Blue	301	389	316	141	352	415	380	430	600	3324		431	558	505	191	401	225	354	377	377	3419	6743		
White	293	379	306	134	344	395	369	393	565	3178		421	499	477	184	383	213	342	368	357	3244	6422		
White/Gold										2970											3063	6033		
Gold	290	345	296	109	333	308	320	305	478	2784		345	453	389	159	313	171	335	358	335	2858	5642		
Green	285	297	291	95	271	306	250	299	472	2566		302	443	356	148	275	166	275	340	330	2635	5201		
Maura																						13		
Shirley																						18		
Par	4	4	4	3	4	4	4	4	5	36		4	5	5	3	4	3	4	4	4	36	72		
Lynn																						22		
Meg																						28		
Men's Handicap	15	5	13	17	7	3	9	1	11			2	4	12	18	6	10	16	8	14				
Women's Handicap	15	5	13	17	1	11	9	3	7			2	4	10	16	14	18	8	6	12				

© Golf ScoreCards, Inc. ©2023 1-800-238-7267

Scorer: _____ Attest: _____ Date: _____

In the second scenario, if they are all playing against par, everyone will get strokes to match their handicaps. Now it gets interesting because, in addition to a stroke for every 18 holes, the player with the 28 handicap is going to get an extra stroke on handicap holes 1-10. Take a look at the scorecard above to see where the double strokes fall.

If you are playing with golfers who are hitting from different tees, you may give or get strokes for that, too. The player hitting from the tees with the higher course rating gets more strokes. To calculate just how many strokes you get, subtract the difference between the course ratings. Let's say there is a 73.5 rating from the middle tees and a 70.9 rating from the forward tees. Subtract 70.9 from the 73.5 rating from the white tees and round up to the nearest decimal from .5. Therefore, the player hitting from the whites would get three extra strokes (74 minus 71).

Now, a bit of true confession. I can write, I can cook, faux paint walls and furniture and grow wonderful plants in my yard. It seems, however, I cannot add very well. This is sadly rooted in my parochial school flashcard experiences, conducted by the Sisters of Mercy – who showed none. As a shy child in grammar school, it was terrifying to stand and deliver answers on math questions while my classmates looked on. If one of us gave an incorrect answer, we were summoned to the front of the class. Out came the wooden ruler to deliver 12 whacks on your open hand. It left me traumatized and deeply embarrassed. Today, I see numbers, but they float around in my mind and then I freeze because I am terrified to make a mistake. So I am always happy to play with a CPA, MBA or any kind of numbers person. The card gets stroked and added once and it is correct. I am eternally grateful to those friends. You know who you are. I shall ever continue to buy you a drink at the 19th hole.

I know all this business about strokes and handicaps sounds a bit confusing at first glance, but it will soon become very routine once you've done it a few times. Once again, take it easy on yourself. Don't worry about this while you are learning. There should be plenty of golf friends in your new social circle now who will help you to learn and support you on your journey.

If you want more information on rules, ESC or any other golf-related verbiage, visit the USGA website or ask your Golf Professional. The Golf Professionals are more than happy to help you to navigate this new area and I promise, there won't be any flash cards or rulers.

"Must you go off and play that wretched game again, darling? Leaving me here, alone and sad, to slave over the microwave oven?"

"Yes, I must. I have promised to make up a foursome."

"Have you no regard for our marriage? Mother did warn me about golfers, but I never thought it would be like this."

"You are being very selfish. I must keep fit. And in any case, the Club Trophy is next month and I am very out of practice."

"One day, you will return and find me gone, the house empty and the children on the streets."

"Yes, well, I must be going now. We must be off by two. I'll be back in time for supper."

Off she goes to the Club and he

returns to the kitchen.

Peter Gammond from "Bluff Your Way in Golf"

Chapter 10

Games to Play While Playing Golf: From Friendly Wagers to Outing Formats

Nassau

The most popular game is called Nassau. You and your fellow players will agree on how much to bet, let's say $2.00 before you tee off. A Nassau is broken into three bets. A player will win $2.00 for the lowest score on the front nine, $2.00 for the lowest score on the back nine, and $2.00 for the lowest score overall. You may play as individuals or as two-person teams. It can be played as Match or Stroke play. The bet is settled at the end of the round, usually at the 19th hole. The most a player can lose is $6. The most you can win is $18.

The Press

No, it's not *The New York Times* asking for an interview. A "press" is just a new bet, most commonly used in a Nassau, that a player can introduce whenever she is two holes down. The original bet stays intact; the press is a side bet and runs concurrently with the game being played. It's a great strategy because if you win the next hole, you now are just one hole down on the original bet, and one up on the Press - the new bet. It could throw your opponent off-balance, especially if you go on to win the second hole, going even on the original bet, and moving to two up on the Press. At that point, your opponents may ask to press because *they* are now two holes down. You should accept the wager if you want to be a good sport. At the end of nine, you had better add up where you are, because if a team loses the front nine, they can press the back nine, making the wager even higher. If it starts looking like they could lose the overall eighteen, they may press the eighteenth hole. Do your bookkeeping faithfully whether you are the collector or the debtor, but don't hold up the foursome behind you. You already know I won't be able to do an accurate accounting. We could be there until the parking lot lights come on.

Best Ball

Sometimes called a four-ball, better ball is a match-play format in which two players compete against two other players. The better score of the two-person team is recorded for each hole, while the higher score for the team is tossed out. For example, if you and your partner each score a four on a par 3, and the other players have a five and a two respectively, the two wins the hole for the opposing team. Your score would be four. Even if you had a stroke for 4 net 3, the player with the 2 still wins the hole. Be sure to stroke your cards to reflect individual handicaps in this game to make it fair.

Six Six Six, Round Robin or COD (Carts, Opposites, Drivers)

Dividing 18 holes by 6 will give you three sets of six holes to compete in a foursome. You will switch partners after every six holes, Six Six Six is just a variation of Better Ball that allows players to play as partners three different times during one round. For the first six holes, the cart partners (Carts) will be a team, in the following six holes, the driver of one cart and the passenger in the other cart (Opposites) will be partners and for the final six holes, the drivers of each cart (Drivers) will be partners. The Better Ball of the team will be used with the appropriate strokes in each instance. Every time a hole is won, the team members will get little dots on the card to reflect the win. The player with the most "dots" at the end of the round is the winner.

Bingo Bango Bongo

A great game for a twosome, threesome and also a foursome. Also referred to as Bingle Bangle Bungle. This is a fun game especially if you have a wide handicap difference in your group because all the "action" happens on the green. A player gets one point for being first on the green, one point for being closest to the hole, and one point for being the first to hole out. You get to decide what the rewards are, be it an amount of money or a round of refreshments at the 19th hole. Some players double the point value if a player wins all three points on a hole. However, players must play according to golf etiquette. Therefore, the player furthest from the hole must always putt first.

Garbage

Hey, I didn't make up these names. Garbage, sometimes called "Trash," (honest!) are side bets. Here are some of the bets you may hear about:

Gross birdies (as opposed to net birdies)

The score you got without using a stroke from your handicap.

Greenies

Whoever gets closest to the hole in regulation on par 3s and 5s.

Sandies

Making par out of the sand.

Barkies

Hitting a tree but still making par.

Hogans (For Ben Hogan)

Hitting the fairway, hitting the green, and making par or better.

Arnies (For Arnold Palmer)

Missing the fairway, missing the green, and still making par or better.

Gurglies

Hitting the ball into the water but still making par.

Offie

A ball holed from off the green.

No doubt you can come up with your own side bets that compare with these in style and creativity.

Nines

Best played with three players. All scores must add up to 9.

A. All 3 players have different scores.

- Best score   5 points
- Second best score   3 points
- Worst score: 1 point

B. One player wins, other best two tie.

- Best score: 5 points
- Second best score tie: 2 points
- Second best score tie: 2 points

C. Two players tie best score.

- Best score tie: 4 points
- Best score tie: 4 points
- Next best: 1 point

D. All players tie.

- Each player: 3 points

Cha Cha Cha

This is such a fun format I learned from my friend, Lynn Tennant. In Cha Cha Cha you will need one best ball on the first hole, two best balls on the second hole and three best balls on the third hole. Get it? One, two cha cha cha! Then on the fourth hole, you are back to one best ball, the fifth hole will require two best balls and the sixth hole will require three best balls. This format keeps you on your toes because everyone in the foursome must contribute.

Skins

Skins is another popular game and can be used with two, three or four players. The annually televised PGA Skins Games, for example, has a large and enthusiastic following.

In a skins game (sometimes referred to as scats or syndicates) the players agree to an amount for each "skin" per hole before the round begins and the players contribute to the pot.

The player with the lowest score on the hole wins a skin.

When you have a "one tie/all tie the result is no skin is won. The value of the tied skin is carried over (added) to the next hole. So whoever wins that next hole wins 2 skins.

Sometimes when a hole is tied, the term "no blood" or "it's a push" may be used, because you are pushing the bet to the next hole.

Wolf

In this classic foursome betting game, a "team" of two can be created on every hole or a daring one-against-three strategy might take place. The hitting order (one through four) is determined on the first tee and will remain in place throughout the round. Players might toss a tee to determine the order of play or pull golf balls from a hat. This order is kept for the entire round. Player #1 will tee off first on the first hole, player #2 will tee off first on the second hole, and player #3 will tee off first on the third hole and player #4 will have the tee on the fourth hole.

The player who tees off first on each hole is the Wolf. The Wolf will then observe the drive of player 2, at which point she will have the option of taking that drive and partnering for the hole or not. She must decide after she has seen the drive. In other words, if Player 2 hits her drive into the rough, The Wolf would pass. If Player 3 hits a bomb down the middle, she might take that player as her partner for that hole, especially if she gets a stroke, and play against players 2 and 4. She cannot wait until Player 4 hits. Whether alone as the Wolf, or with a partner, the side with the "better ball" score wins the hole.

The Wolf may also announce before teeing off that she intends to play the hole alone (the lone wolf) which is most common on Par 3s and 5s.

How to score:

2 teams of 2 players:

The Wolf's team wins the hole. Each team player earns 2 points

The other team beats the Wolf's team: Each team player wins 3 points.

Lone Wolf playing against all other players:

The Wolf beats other players, the Wolf earns 4 points

One player beats the Wolf: All players earn 5 points except the Wolf.

One last comment on Wolf. The 17th and 18th holes are "leftover" holes so the player in last place is usually given the courtesy of teeing off first and being the Wolf on the final two holes. Very civilized indeed.

Scramble

The Scramble has become the format of choice for many charity outings because it speeds play for a large field and allows less accomplished players to participate without undue pressure.

In a Scramble, all the players drive off the tee, then the best drive is selected. All players hit their second shot from that spot, and so on until the ball is holed. With the Mulligans that are often sold, a team could potentially come in well under par.

One way to make a Scramble a little harder for 18 holes is to require each player's drive to be used twice. Or the person whose drive is used must step aside on the second shot.

Chapman/Alternate Shot

This is a great format when you have a couples event or if you are having a Solheim tournament at your club. In this format, there are teams of two. Both players drive and then each hits the other's ball for the second shot. Select the best of the two second shots, then play into the hole, alternating shots. Remember, if your ball stops one inch from the cup, your partner must tap it in. Jokingly referred to as "The Divorce Open" when used as a "Couples Cup" format, I have seen many sullen faces return to the club house for dinner as hostilities are set aside until later at home. It could take days for relationships to return to normal.

"Please shut up," the husband snapped at his nagging wife during their Couples Cup golf tournament. "You are driving me out of my mind."

"That," she retorted, "wouldn't be a drive. It would just be a short putt."

Robert McCune from *The World's Best Golf Jokes*

Stableford

Another interesting tournament format is Stableford, whereby point values are attached to scores. For example, a bogey gets one point, par is two points, a birdie is three points, and an eagle is awarded four points. The player with the most points at the end of the round wins.

This a good game to speed play because if you are over a bogie, you are not getting any points, so you can just move to the next hole. Write down what you estimate you would have gotten for a score on that hole (ESC). Stableford rewards the player with the most points rather than the player with the lowest score.

The Rope

Each player is given a length of thin rope and a pair of kindergarten-style scissors. You know, the plastic ones with the rounded ends. We can't have any puncture wounds during the round. For example, let's say each player is given 10 feet of rope. Should you land in the bunker but are close to the edge, you may move the ball out of the bunker and place it on the grass. If you need 2 feet to accomplish this task, then you must cut off 2 feet from your rope. The rope comes in most handy on the green. If you are 4 feet from the cup, you may call it holed but then you must cut 4 feet from your rope.

Regardless of what games you are playing, when you make your "bookkeeping entries" on your scorecard to keep track of all bets out, be sure you are not delaying play for the folks behind you. One last thing, be sure to pay off your debt immediately after the round.

If you would like some additional information on games within the game, visit PGA.com. There are also many books on the market to give you endless ideas for fun and challenging games within the game.

"A bad day on the golf course:
You run over your own foot with your cart.
Other golfers call you "Shank".
Your shoes have enough sand in them to open a beach.
The rest of your foursome huddles behind a bench when you
tee off.
Your tee time for tomorrow has been revoked.
Your woods are too embarrassed to come out of the bag.
The course superintendent threatens you with legal action.
Birds flying south readjust their flight pattern when you hit."
Richard Mintzer, from *The Unofficial Golfer's Handbook*

Glossary

Ace
Into the hole in one stroke: a hole in one.

Addressing the ball
The position taken just before you hit.

Adjusted score
Your gross score minus your handicap

Aeration
Poking holes into the turf every few inches from tee to green to allow for better air circulation in the soil underneath the turf.

Albatross
Another name for a double Eagle.

Alternate Shot
One player hits the drive, the second player hits the second shot. This format continues until the hole is completed.

All square
A match that is tied between two opposing sides.

Approach
A short or medium shot played to the putting green or pin. Also called Approach Shot.

Apron
The short grass around the green, also called the collar or fringe.

Attest
Signing your scorecard as testimony that what you recorded for your hole to hole score, and final score, is true.

Away
The golfer who is farthest from the hole is considered to be away.

Back Door
A putt that is holed by rolling along the rim to the back side of the cup and then dropping in.

Backspin
A reverse spin a player can put on a ball in flight which prevents it from bouncing forward after landing on the green. Could also be referred to as "bite".

Baseball Grip
Holding the club without interlocking the fingers.

Beach
Slang for sand trap/bunker.

Best Ball
A match format in which the better ball score from two balls or the best score from four balls is recorded for each hole.

Birdie
A score of one under par on any hole.

Bite
See Backspin. Or a plea issued by a player to the ball, begging it to stop once it hits the green, but appears to be rolling past the hole.

Blast
A bunker shot used when the ball is buried in the sand. The unfortunate position of the ball is also referred to as "a fried egg".

Blind Hole
A hole where the green cannot be seen from the tee box.

Bogey
A score of one over par.

Brain Cramp
When all of your previous golf learning and experience abandons your cerebral area, and you have absolutely no idea how you just botched that shot.

Break
The undulations on the green, subtle or not, which must be studied so that a player can "read" the break and select a target line before putting.

Bump and Run
An approach shot that is hit low and long. It is often useful from off the green or might be the most practical shot to get back into play from deep in the woods.

Bunker
A hole filled with sand, aka a sand trap. You may not ground your club in a bunker.

Caddy
A person who carries a player's bag. An experienced caddie will offer advice about the course, club selection, discuss strategies for shots. A caddie will clean your ball, rake the bunkers, replace your divots and keep your clubs clean between shots. A great caddie will keep you calm and focused, make sure you stay hydrated and even give you the score for just about any sports event from his or her cell phone while you are on the golf course.

Carry
The distance a ball must travel from the place where you hit it and where it lands. For example, a caddie might tell you that "this hole is all carry". Good players know exactly how much each club

carries. Hopefully, we will all remember to take a bit more club to cover the "carry'.

Casual Water
Any body of water that is not part of the course 365 days a year. For example, a puddle in the fairway after a hard rain. Players may take penalty-free relief. (See Rules) Dew and frost are not considered casual water.

Chili-dip
To hit the ball fat, most often with a wedge.

Chip
A short approach shot made from around the green using a lofted club to get the ball up in the air and onto the green.

Choke down
Also referred to as grip down. It means holding your club lower on the grip. Honestly, I do not use the word "choke" in any way related to golf. We never want to "choke" under pressure.

Cleek
An old term for a 4-wood.

Closed face
For right-handed players, having the club face turned slightly to the slightly left at address.

Closed stance
At address, a right-handed player will have the left toe line moved slightly over the parallel line with the target, while the right foot will be in line with the target. Often used to solve a slicing problem.

Course Rating
The comparison of one course to another in terms of diffuculty. The higher the rating, the more difficult the course.

Cup
The hole on the green.

Dance floor
Slang for the green. If you are far away from the hole, you are on the dance floor but not close to the band.

Divot
A piece of turf dug out when the club head hits down on the the ball during the swing. Be sure to either replace the divot (if you live in climates where replaced divots will grow back) or fill the hole with the sand/seed mixture provided on your golf cart. This is one of the Cardinal Rules of golf. Replacing or filling divots allows the turf to repair itself and stay in top condition. Sadly, no relief from divots when playing in a tournament. Happily, relief from divots when you are new to golf.

Dogleg
The name given to any hole which bends dramatically to the right or left.

Dormie
The term given to the situation in Match Play when a competitor is ahead by the number of holes left to play. For example, Andy is three up with three to play. Borrowed from Latin and French words meaning "to sleep".

Double Bogey
A score of two over par for a single hole.

Double Eagle
Three strokes less than par.

Double Par
Twice the par for the hole. Time to pick up if playing a casual round.

Down

A term used to describe where a player is in a Match. For example, "I am down by four." A Match is played hole-by-hole, so don't get too upset if you are down a few holes in the early part of the Match.

Draw

A skillful, controlled shot that curves to the left for a right-handed player. Also can refer to the pairing of golfers for a Match play tournament.

Drive

The first shot taken from the tee at each hole.

Dub

A missed or poorly-struck shot.

Duff

A mis-hit.

Duffer

An unskilled golfer. Also known as a hacker.

Eagle

A score of two under par on a hole.

Executive Golf Course

A bit shorter than a standard golf course, it may offer 9 or 18 holes. It has a lower par because it generally has more Par 3s than a standard golf course, but may still offer a few Par 4s and 5s. These are great facilities for beginners and juniors, or anyone who is short on time but long on desire to get a few holes in.

Fade

A skillful, controlled (unlike a slice) shot to a target that curves slightly from left to right for a right-handed player.

Fairway
The lush, grassy part of the golf course that is cut shorter than the rough.

Fat
An expression used when you hit well behind the ball. You might say you hit the big ball (planet earth) before you hit the little white ball. Can also be called thick, fat, chunky or heavy.

Fellow Competitor
In stroke/medal play, it is the relationship between players.

Fescue
An unpleasant form of grass used a the "rough" on many courses.

Flag stick
A pole with a flag on it which tells players where the cup/hole location is on the green. Often color-coded flags are used to tell players that the cup is located, e.g. at the front (red), middle (white) or back of the green (blue). The flag stick is also referred to as the pin.

Flight
Term used to group players by similar handicap when playing in a league or large tournament. For example: Flight A has Scratch through 9-handicaps, Flight B has 10 through 19-handicaps and Flight C has 20 through 29-handicaps.

In addition, flight is used to describe a ball in the air; it is said "to be in flight".

Follow-through
Finishing your swing after impact.

Fore!
A loud verbal warning you must yell with gusto to warn other golfers near you that an errant shot is coming their way.

Four Ball
Match competition in which the better ball of two players is played against the better ball of their opponents.

Free Lift
Moving your ball without penalty. See Rules.

Fried Egg
A ball semi-buried in a bunker.

Fringe
The short grass around the green, also called the "apron" or "collar".

General Area
New term which has replaced "through the green". The General Area covers the entire course except: the teeing area, bunkers, penalty areas and the putting green.

Get Legs
A plea to encourage your golf ball to keep rolling when you suspect it is going to stop short.

Get up and down
Making par after a challenging shot or two. For example, your tee shot was errant, but you got back into a good position on your second shot. Your third shot landed near the pin and you made the 6' putt for par.

GHIN
Golf Handicap Information Network. The governing body for the handicap system in the US.

Gimme

A putt so close to the hole that your playing partners allow you to pick it up, but the stroke must be counted, Gimmes are not recognized by the Rules of Golf, but are quite common in casual rounds. It is widely considered to be a friendly gesture and it helps to keep play moving along.

Grain

The direction the blades of the grass grow on a green. For example, if there is a pond nearby, it will grow toward the water. The grain will play a role in how fast or slowly your putt will roll. You will be "with" or "against" the grain.

Green fee

The price set by a golf club for a round of golf. It does not necessarily include cart cost.

Grip

How you place your hands on the top of the club where the leather resides.

Gross score

Your total score before subtracting your handicap to arrive at your net score.

Grounding the Club

Touching the ground behind your ball with your club head before you hit, The only "no-no" concerning grounding the club happens in bunkers where it will earn you a two-stroke penalty.

Ground under repair

An area on the course that is off-limits to players because it is unfit for play. Usually marked by white paint or roped off with a GUR sign. It is a free lift, no closer to the hole for players.

Half or halved hole or Match
In Match play, a hole or Match that is tied. The term "no blood" or "push" is also used in this instance.

Handicap
A number assigned to amateur players based on the most recent 20 scores posted on the USGA GHIN system. Using the best 10 scores, it numerically categorizes playing ability by taking into consideration the overall difficulty of the course and its difficulty for a scratch or a bogey golfer. Your handicap estimates roughly how close to par you are expected to shoot on any golf course. The handicap is the game's great equalizer in that players get strokes so that they can compete on even terms with better players.

Hard pan
A flat, hard and dried out area with little or no turf.

Heeled shot
A shot hit off the heel of your club.

Hit a house
A term used when a shot is hit too firmly and the ball goes speeding by the hole. Similar to hit a brick. If you ever find a golf ball that actually listens, put me down for a dozen!

Holing Out
To complete the play for one hole by hitting the ball into the cup.

Honor
The right to tee off first because you have won the previous hole or the obligation on the first tee if you have the lowest handicap in your foursome.

Hook
A wild shot that goes sharply from right to left for right-handed players.

Hosel
The opening where the shaft is attached and then glued into the club head.

Index
The portable number on your GHIN card used to compute your handicap when playing various courses and represents your playing ability.

Inside the Leather
A phrase used when a putt is considered to be shorter than the length of the leather grip on a putter. It's a hint for a gimme.

Knee knocker
A short putt that is critically needed to win a hole or a match. Most players are afraid they will miss even before they address the ball. Remember what Kathy Hart Wood told us about the Three Cs.

Lag
A long putt that is stroked to stop hopefully within a few inches of the cup. Sometimes, they even drop into the cup.

Layup shot
Playing a shot short of the target to stay out of trouble, especially around penalty areas. Shows good course management skills if a player lacks the skill or confidence to execute a difficult shot.

Lie
Where your ball comes to rest after a shot, e.g. "You have a very good lie." Also, the current number of strokes taken on a hole, e.g. "I lie four." In addition, is it what you might do on the 19th hole to describe your round!

Line

The path the ball must travel on the green in order to go into the hole. Quite often, you will hear someone say, "You had the right line, but not enough distance."

Links

A style of golf course that is built along a coastline, buffeted by strong winds. No significant changes are made to the land and courses are largely treeless with sandy soil. Nothing grows in that soil except tall, thick native grasses. Tee boxes and greens are constructed and fairways are cut just like any other course, but just about everything around it is found in a natural state with a very undulating topography. Bunkers are very deep to prevent sand from blowing away. Pete Dye was famous for his links designs, and many courses in Europe are links style. A fine example of a links course is St. Andrew's in Scotland. Links has come to mean any golf course, when players say, "Let's hit the links".

Lip

The edge of the hole. For example, a player might comment, "It lipped out.", when referring to a putt that flirted with the hole by circling the opening, but not dropping in.

Local Rules

Rules a golf club will set to govern play on its course in addition to following the Rules of Golf.

Loft

The angle of the club face. A driver can range from 8 to 13 degrees, while a wedge can be as high as 60 degrees. Loft may also describe the elevation of the ball in flight.

Long irons

The 1-, 2-, and 3- irons.

Loose Impediments
Any natural object that is not fixed or growing. Includes stones, twigs, branches, molehills, animal dung, worms and insects.

Lost Ball
Any ball that is not found and identified within 3 minutes of searching.

LPGA
Ladies Professional Golf Association

Marker
Small round disk or coin used to identify the location of your ball on the green. To mark your ball, place the marker behind your ball without moving it or touching it. Once marked, you may pick your ball up to clean it.

Markers
The objects placed at the tee boxes to indicate where players must tee their ball. For example, there are Red markers, Green, Gold, White, Blue and Black markers.

Match play
A form of competition in which the number of holes won determines the winner, rather than the lowest score.

Medal play
Count all strokes; the lowest Gross score wins. Also referred to as Stroke play. This is the most difficult type of competition because it is possible to get a very high score on a hole. For example, if your third shot goes into the water on a Par five you will lie 5 with the penalty stroke, should your next shot go in as well, you are now lying 8. You might need 2 or three more shots to finish the hole. No matter how many more shots you need to finish the hole, you have to count all of them.

Middle irons
The 4-, 5- and 6-irons

Mulligan
Not recognized by the USGA, and never used in real competition.
It is a shot replayed (without counting the previous stroke) when a
player's first shot is a disaster. In a casual round of golf, a group
might agree at the first hole that one mulligan per side is okay.
Mulligans are often sold at charity events to raise money.

Nassau
A Match play format whereby players wager on three things:
winning the front nine, winning the back nine and winning overall.

Net score
The final score after deducting the handicap from the gross score.

Nineteenth hole
After the round, players head for the bar for refreshments, food and
conversation. Scores are added, bets are settled and stories are
exchanged, usually about the best and worst shots of the round.

Ninety Degree Rule/90 degree rule
Golf carts are allowed to drive on the fairway or away from cart
paths only perpendicularly (90 degrees) to decrease wear and tear
on the course or to protect fragile grass.

OB
Out-of-bounds: the area lying outside of the defined golf course.
Marked by white stakes or lines on the course. Stroke and distance
penalty. Please refer to Rules for more information.

Open stance
For a right-handed player at address, the left foot is set slightly
behind the imaginary line to the target, the right foot on the target
line.

Par
The number of strokes required to finish a hole in regulation. Holes have a par of 3, 4 or 5.

Penalty Area
Defined by red or yellow lines or stakes.

Penalty stroke
When you break a rule, you have to add a penalty stroke, or two, to your score depending on the seriousness of your infraction. Please see Rules for more information.

Pick Up
To drop out of a hole by picking up your ball before holing out.

PGA
Professional Golfer's Association

Pin
A commonly used term for the flag stick.

Pin High
Referring to a ball that is on the green and even with the pin, but off to either side of the pin.

Pitch
An approach shot to the green using a lofted club to play over a short distance with a steep ascent and descent. A pitch shot will travel farther than a chip shot, with less roll.

Pitch and putt course
Shorter than an executive course, usually 9 Par 3 holes. A great place for beginners or to work on your short game.

Play it down
You must play the ball where it lies. Also referred to as Summer Rules.

Play it up
You may roll the ball over for a better lie. Also referred to as Winter Rules. You may not lift, clean and place.

Play through
If the group ahead of you is playing slowly, and a hole or two holes ahead of them are open, they should invite you to play through. They will step aside, let you tee off and resume their play after you are out of range. Do not hesitate to ask to play through under these circumstances or call the Pro Shop or Ranger and ask for assistance. It is considered rude to simply jump ahead of the group without some form of conversation and agreement. Murphy's Law dictates that when playing through, one tends to play badly.

Plugged lie
A common occurrence whenever the ground is very wet. Imagine your ball is embedded in the ground after your shot. You have some options: play it where it lies, no penalty. Move it if it's in casual water, no penalty. If the course has a local rule, you may lift, clean and place it, no closer to the hole, penalty free. If none of the above situations exist, you can declare it unplayable, drop, and take a one stroke penalty. The only instance where you may not declare your ball unplayable is in a Penalty Area. Then you have an Unplayable Lie and will need to use the Stroke and Distance one stroke penalty.

Pot bunker
A sand trap that is very deep. At St. Andrew's there are ladders that players use to climb in and out.

Preferred lie
When winter rules are in effect as posted by the Pro Shop, usually following a severe storm that has caused muddy playing conditions,

a player may move the ball and/or lift, clean and place to improve her lie by one club length no closer to the hole. Preferred lies are not recognized by the Rules of Golf.

Pre-shot routine
Any procedure which mentally and physically prepares the player to hit the ball. The most common pre-shot routine is a practice swing.

Pro-Am
A tournament, usually for charity, in which professional golfers (Pro) play with amateur golfers (Am).

Provisional Ball
The playing of a second ball from the same place as the first because the player is unsure of what may have happened to the first ball.

Pull
A shot that travels left of the target for right-handed players.

Punch shot
If you find yourself under some low tree branches, try a punch shot to get back into play. Use a low iron, close the club head a bit and hit the ball off your back foot to keep it low. Hopefully, you were firm enough with your short back swing "punch" to get the ball out of trouble.

Push
A poor shot that moves to the right of the target for right-handed players. Want to stop doing that? Make a date with your Golf Professional!

Putt Line
The path your ball must follow to go from where it lies on the green into the hole. Please be mindful of other player's putt line when

you are on the green. It is considered discourteous to walk on another player's putt line.

Rain maker
A popped-up shot off the tee that goes high into the sky but not very far.

Ranger
An employee of the golf course who patrols the course to keep the pace of play moving smoothly. The Ranger has the authority to revoke the privileges of individuals who are intentionally hitting into other players or being a nuisance on the golf course.

Ready golf
An agreement among players that speeds play because players hit when ready, assuming it is safe to do so, rather than waiting for the player who is "away".

Recovery shot
A difficult or risky shot made from an area of trouble, such as heavy rough or a stand of trees, that gets a player back into play.

Relief
If your ball rolls into casual water or ends up on a cart path, you are entitled to penalty free relief. See Rules.

Rider
When a new golfer hits the ball far enough to warrant actually getting into the cart and "riding" to the next shot.

Rough
The longer, dense grass on the golf course on either side of the fairway.

Rub of the Green
Term used to define a ball in flight accidentally stopped or deflected by an outside agency such as an observer, a fore caddie, a cart or a sprinkler head. No penalty is incurred but you must play the ball where it lies. Rub of the green can work both ways. For example, if your ball hits a mower/tractor and goes into the water, that is bad luck. However, if your ball hits the mower/tractor and ends up on the green and just a few feet from the hole, that is good luck. Good luck is sometimes called a "member's bounce".

Sandbagger
Not a flattering term. It implies one is a skilled player who keeps his or her handicap artificially inflated to gain a competitive advantage by getting extra strokes.

Sand trap
Another name for a bunker.

Scotch foursome
A form of competition for men and women. They are a team of either two or four, playing the same ball but alternating shots into the cup. Can be played over 9 or 18 holes.

Scramble
An outing format as well as a term used when someone gets out of trouble to save par. As an outing format, teams of two or four players continuously pick the best shot. Then all players hit from that location until the ball is holed.

Scratch player
A person with a zero handicap, shooting even par.

Scuff
A shot hit thin or a mark on the cover of your ball, especially if it has hit the cart path.

Set up
Your posture, alignment and ball position at address.

Shamble
Just as in a Scramble, all members of the foursome tee off and the best drive of the group is selected. All players will now play their own balls into the hole from there.

Shank
Frankly, this is one of the most feared words in golf. It is right up there in its ability to strike terror into the hearts of players as the word "yips." A shank is just a terrible miss-hit when the ball is not actually hit by the clubface, but off the hosel and ricochets right for a right-handed player. The hosel is the part of the club that joins the club head to the shaft. In early golfing times, that part of the club used to be called the shank.

Short game
The part of the game that begins about 100 yards from the green. This is when skillful use of wedges, accurate chipping and putting are critical to a good score.

Short irons
The 7-, 8-, and 9-irons and all wedges.

Shotgun start
A competition format that allows all contenders to start at different holes on the course at the same time, thus allowing everyone to finish at the same time.

Skins
A wager which moves from hole to hole with the lowest score winning. In the event of a tie on a given hole, the skin just rolls over until a player wins the next hole outright.

Skulled

To "skull" the ball means contact is first made with the leading edge of the iron or wedge which results in a ball hit in the middle rather than underneath. The ball screams off on a low trajectory with no spin. Players may also refer to it as "blading the shot" or "hitting it thin".

Slice

An out-of-control shot that goes sharply off to the right for a right-handed player. A slice is the most common ailment for amateur golfers. It is the result of a number of things a player is doing incorrectly, and is best remedied by a lesson with your Golf Professional.

Slope

Used by the USGA to measure the difficulty of a course for the average golfer.

Spoon

An old term for a 3-wood.

Square

A term for a match that is all even, or a term regarding a golfer's stance that is lined up properly to the target line. You will hear the term "square up" from your Instructor many times.

Square face

The correct club head position for most golf shots. On some occasions, a player will want to close the face to keep the ball low or open the face to create more loft.

Stableford

A scoring method that uses points instead of strokes. A player might get 1 point for a bogey, 2 points for par, 3 points for a birdie and so on.

Stance

The feet position when addressing the ball. An Instructor may suggest you widen or narrow your stance, for example.

Starter
The person at the golf course responsible for signaling players to come to the first tee when it is their turn to tee off.

Stimpmetre
A device used by golf course Superintendents to measure the speed of the green. The readings give a "snapshot" of the green speed at that time of the day. If you have ever heard someone ask how the greens are "stimping" on any given day, they are asking what to expect out on the course. Greens running or stimping at five to six are slow, seven to eight means a medium speed while greens stimping at nine to ten are going to be fast. Any number over eleven and you will find yourself in the PGA/LPGA Tournament league of super fast greens. Usually the Starter will tell you how the greens are running first thing in the morning, but keep in mind, as the day wears on, the sun dries them out and that will affect speed. Also, the grass will grow just a bit by late afternoon, so what was super fast in the am might be a tad more sluggish later in the day. Greens are cut and rolled with care to get those speeds up for tournament play, but many egronomists will argue that to maintain such levels of speed daily can stress a green and cause damage.

Stroke and distance
A penalty. It means that you must add one penalty stroke to your score and lose the distance your ball traveled. Please see Rules for details for a new way to play Stroke and Distance with a two stroke penalty which eliminates "the distance'.

Stroke hole
The holes where a player receives a handicap stroke on the scorecard.

Stroke play

Same as Medal play. All balls must be holed on all holes. A player may not pick up. The lowest score wins.

Swale

A moderate dip in the terrain. Not as deep as a ditch or a ravine. Your ball did not disappear on the fairway. It landed in a swale.

Sweet spot

An area on every club face which, when proper contact is made with the ball, results in the best shot in terms of direction, control and distance.

Swing speed

Measured in miles per hour, it reveals how fast the club head is moving at impact with the ball.

Take away

Refers to the beginning of your back swing.

Tee

The peg, made of wood or plastic, which is used to place your ball on for your tee shot. Also refers to the tee box. Did you know in "the old days" golfers would build a tiny pile of sand to elevate the ball for driving.

Tee box

The area reserved at each hole where a player may tee the ball up. Usually designated by two parallel markers facing the fairway. A player may not tee up outside of the markers.

Tempo

Refers to the speed/rhythm with which you swing your club.

Temporary Green
A green used in winter to save the permanent green. In winter climates, greens are covered to protect them against damage from ice and snow. Before the snow flies, some intrepid golfers want to get as many rounds in as possible, so the temporary greens help them to get the most out of being outside in 30 degree temperatures. If you are a Floridian, there is simply no explanation for this level of dedication to the game.

Texas wedge
This is the term used when a putter is used for a shot from off the green or from a sand trap that has a very low lip.

Thin shot
A ball hit just slightly in the middle or on the top, rather than getting under it with the club head.

Through the green
An old phrase recently replaced with "General Area".

Toed shot
A shot which hits the golf ball off the toe of the club face. The ball will hop along the ground rather than become airborne.

Topping the ball.
Hitting the ball above its center. A skulled or thin shot.

Trajectory
The ball's height and flight pattern after being hit.

Trap
A bunker.

Triple bogey
Three strokes over par.

Under club
A common ailment among amateurs. It means a player has not selected the right club from the bag to hit the ball the distance it needs to travel "on the fly" to get to the target, usually the green. In other words, a player used a 7-iron rather than a 6-iron. Wind direction and elevation play a big role in club selections as well.

Unplayable lie
A ball that cannot be hit due to interference from a tree, fence or other unmovable obstruction. Take a one stroke penalty and refer to the Rules Chapter for complete instructions about how to get back into play.

Up
The number of strokes you are ahead of your opponent in Match play.

Up and Down
Getting out of trouble on a hole from a Penalty Area or Bunker and into the hole. You will often hear a player say, "That was a good up and down."

USGA

United States Golf Association. Established 1894. Also used by players to tease someone in the foursome by saying, "USGA: Ugly shot, go again."

Vardon grip

The most widely used golf grip whereby, for right-handed players, the pinkie finger of the right hand is inserted between the index and middle finger of the left hand. This type of grip is touted by many to offer the most comfort and control.

Waggle
The little back and forth motion a player makes at address with the club head, just before the takeaway. Many players "waggle" just to keep their hands relaxed and to offer a kind of trigger before starting the swing.

WGAM
Women's Golf Association of Massachusetts. The oldest state women's golf association in the country having been established in 1900. Some days I feel like that is the year I started playing golf!

Whiff
Every golfer's nightmare. It means that the ball is completely missed when trying to hit it. Sadly, it counts as a stroke and is one of golf's most humbling experiences.

Windcheater
A solidly hit shot that stays low to "cheat" the wind from slowing it down. It rises only toward the end of the shot.

Winter rules
When winter rules are in effect, a player may "play the ball up" by moving it from its lie in the fairway. Not recognized by the USGA.

Worm burner
A poorly hit shot that rolls along the ground. Tell the worms to keep their heads down.

Wrist cock or wrist hinge
During the back swing, the wrists "hinge" which is one way to create more power when the player releases the hinge during the downswing and just before impact.

Waste Bunker
Waste bunkers are natural sandy areas, usually very large and most often found on links courses. Waste Bunkers are not considered

"Penalty Areas" according to the Rules of Golf, so you are allowed to ground your club in them and also remove loose impediments (twigs, stones and leaves, etc.) near your ball.

Yips
An ailment that afflicts some players on the green. It is the inability to put a smooth stroke on the ball.

About the Author

Cheryl Nicolazzo has been a passionate leader in the field of golf for professional women for many years. She has been featured in publications such as Time Magazine, Golf Digest and Entrepreneur magazines and has appeared on both television and radio.

Encouraging professional women to use golf as a business tool, she has worked with companies like Fidelity Investments, Ford Motor Company, General Electric Aircraft Engines, Merrill Lynch and Pepsi Bottling Company. She has a background in international trade and business as an executive with Bank Boston and later as President and COO of The International Business Center of New England.

She graduated cum laude from Harvard University. Cheryl divides her time between Woodland Golf Club in Newton, MA and Palmira Golf and Country Club in Bonita Springs, FL with her husband, Nick and their mini-poodle, Sophie.

Cheryl Nicolazzo

Made in the USA
Columbia, SC
19 October 2024